NORTHERN LIGHTS

NORTHERN LIGHTS

The Positive Policy Example of
Sweden, Finland, Denmark and Norway

ANDREW SCOTT

MONASH University Publishing

Monash University Publishing
Matheson Library and Information Services Building
40 Exhibition Walk
Monash University
Clayton, Victoria 3800, Australia
www.publishing.monash.edu

Monash University Publishing brings to the world publications which advance the best traditions of humane and enlightened thought.

Monash University Publishing titles pass through a rigorous process of independent peer review.

www.publishing.monash.edu/books/nl-9781921867927.html

Series: Public Policy

Design: Les Thomas

Cover photograph: Fredrik Broms

National Library of Australia Cataloguing-in-Publication entry:

Creator:	Scott, Andrew, 1963 – author.
Title:	Northern lights : the positive policy example of Sweden, Finland, Denmark and Norway / Andrew Scott.
ISBN:	9781921867927 (paperback)
Notes:	Includes index.
Subjects:	Comparative government.
	Australia--Politics and government.
	Scandinavia--Politics and government.
	Australia--Social policy.
	Scandinavia--Social policy.
	Scandinavia--Economic policy.
	Scandinavia--Economic conditions.
	Scandinavia--Social conditions.
	Scandinavia--Environmental conditions.
	Australia--Social conditions.
Dewey Number:	330.948

Printed in Australia by Griffin Press an Accredited ISO AS/NZS 14001:2004 Environmental Management System printer.

The paper this book is printed on is certified against the Forest Stewardship Council ® Standards. Griffin Press holds FSC chain of custody certification SGS-COC-005088. FSC promotes environmentally responsible, socially beneficial and economically viable management of the world's forests.

CONTENTS

In memory of my brother-in-law,
Corrado Robert D'Ambrosio
(3 April 1963 – 29 December 2013),

who would have liked to see the Northern Lights

ACKNOWLEDGEMENTS

Earlier versions of some of the material in this book appeared in the *Australian Review of Public Affairs* and the *Scandinavian Journal of History*. Thank you to Deakin University for granting me academic study leave from January to July 2014 to finish writing the book, and particularly to Matthew Clarke for his support for that. Thanks also to the Monash University European and EU Centre for hosting me as a visiting scholar during that period.

In my three intensive research visits to the Nordic nations since 2007, I have been fortunate to have had extremely helpful guides. Those whom I have directly quoted, from interviews which I conducted with them – like those whom I interviewed in Australia – are mentioned in the appropriate footnote(s), and I thank them all collectively here. Those whom I have not explicitly quoted from interviews but who nevertheless gave me very valuable assistance, I thank individually here: Jenny Andersson, Elisabeth Elgán, Mary Hilson, Staffan Janson, Åke Sandberg, Tapio Salonen, R. Jakob Munch, Mikkel Mailand, Vibe Westh, Lone Henriksen, Mathias Askholm, Cecilie Kisling, Tony Kallevig, Steinar Holden, Ole Andreas Engen, Ingrid Hjort, Torben Mideksa, Karl Ove Moene and Halvor Mehlum.

For encouraging my initial research into Nordic nations' policy lessons for Australia, I thank Gabrielle Meagher, Sean Scalmer, John Langmore, Philomena Murray, Natalie Doyle and Pascaline Winand. For helping my research into past policy interest in the Nordic nations, I thank George Koletsis, Laurie Carmichael, Dave Oliver, Geoff Dow, Russell Lansbury, Stuart Macintyre, Max Ogden,

Julius Roe, Iain Campbell and the late Ted Wilshire. I also thank the staff of the Swedish Metal Workers' Union for assisting me with access to its archives, the staff of the Labour Movement Archives and Library in Stockholm and of the Noel Butlin Archives Centre in Canberra. For supporting and helping to better inform my initiatives on Nordic lessons for children's policy in Australia, thank you to Mike Salvaris, Lance Emerson, Fiona Stanley, Megan Leuenberger, Sharon Goldfeld, Deborah Brennan and Peter Whiteford. I am grateful to Jacqueline Lo and the Australian National University Centre for European Studies for enabling my participation in a workshop with Pasi Sahlberg in 2012; and to Angelo Gavrielatos of the Australian Education Union and Gabrielle Leigh of the Victorian Principals' Association, for helping me make contact with their Finnish counterparts. Thanks also to Nick Koletsis and Roy Green; and to the ACTU's Grant Belchamber for sharing his experience of studying Danish 'Flexicurity'. I am also grateful to photographer Fredrik Broms for allowing me to use the striking picture he took, from near where he lives in Tromsø, Norway, of the astronomical phenomenon which is the Northern Lights, which appears on this book's front cover. Thank you too to cartographer Erin Koletsis for the map which she custom-made. That map's representation of the Norwegian oilfields in the North Sea draws on 2014 data from the website of the Norwegian Petroleum Directorate at http://www.npd.no/en/, which is gratefully acknowledged.

Nathan Hollier as publisher has been a very generous supporter of this project. I extend my utmost gratitude to him for his interest and his very detailed and intelligent input drawing on his considerable expertise as an editor. My long-standing friend since 1981 and fellow Richmond Football Club (Tigers) supporter, Richard McPhee, has

ACKNOWLEDGEMENTS

read the manuscript in detail as I have proceeded and has made many very helpful criticisms as well as giving many much appreciated encouragements. Younger, postgraduate academics Freda Haylett and Tej Boddupalli have also made very helpful comments. Thanks too, as always, to all my family. None of the above, however, is responsible for the opinions or interpretation presented, which are my own and for which I take full responsibility.

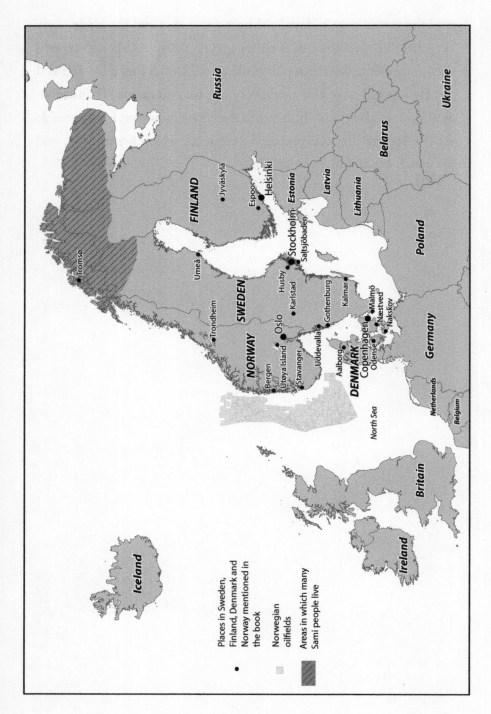

Places in Sweden,
Finland, Denmark and
Norway mentioned in
the book

Norwegian
oilfields

Areas in which many
Sami people live

NOTE ON CURRENCY REFERENCES AND CONVERSION RATES

All references to dollars ($) in this book are to Australian dollars.

All overseas currency conversions are calculated according to the Australian dollar buy rate in the retail exchange market on day 1 of the 2014–2015 financial year as published in the *Australian Financial Review* newspaper on that day.

Therefore, one Australian dollar is calculated to equal 6.5609 Swedish kronor, 5.3758 Danish kroner and 5.9881 Norwegian kroner.

Finland uses the Euro (€) currency, but no direct comparisons between Finland's spending in Euros and Australia's spending in dollars are made in this book, so no precise conversion rate needs to be identified.

INTRODUCTION

People in English-speaking countries who are concerned about rising inequalities have frequently looked to Sweden and its neighbours as offering a policy approach which combines economic prosperity with comparative social equality. The interest has ranged from British Fabians and a noted American journalist in the 1930s to Australian trade unionists and a Canadian politics academic in the 1980s. In more recent decades, such admiration has dissipated due to an impression that comprehensive welfare provision in the Nordic nations is in retreat and that policy options for smaller nation states have been reduced by 'globalisation'.

A trade-union initiated discussion during the 1980s in Australia, focusing on Sweden's achievement of full employment and wage solidarity, for instance, evaporated following the international economic setbacks of the early 1990s due to an inaccurate perception that the entire 'Swedish model' had collapsed. Policy interest in the continuing evident achievements of Sweden and the other Nordic nations has gradually re-emerged in Australia since then, though in a somewhat different way to before. The interest this time has come not so much from unionists and industrial relations scholars, as from social policy activists and academics and educationalists. They have been attracted particularly by the Nordic nations' successes in upholding gender equality, providing substantial welfare, protecting the rights and needs of children and achieving excellence in schools in a fair and inclusive way.

The term 'Scandinavia' includes Sweden, Norway and Denmark, while the term 'Nordic' includes those countries and also Finland.

This book is written in the belief that the nations of Scandinavia and Finland, or Nordic Europe, *do* continue to provide important living proof that economically successful, socially fair and environmentally responsible policies can succeed. My own belief in this has strengthened, and my interest in expressing it has endured, over several years of research. In part this is because a case for adopting different policies is stronger if those policies can be shown to be working in practice than if the case is just argued from abstract principles.

The four principal Nordic nations – Sweden, Finland, Denmark and Norway – have a combined population size of approximately 25 million, which is similar to Australia's population size of approximately 23 million. (Iceland is the other i.e. the fifth Nordic nation. It has a very small population of approximately 320,000 and will not be included in this study.)

The four main Nordic nations are consistently assessed as being among the most economically prosperous and innovative nations in the world.[1] They also still rate as the most equitable nations in terms of income distribution. There remains strong evidence of economic and social achievement in Nordic nations, maintained by policies which continue to be more recognisably social democratic than elsewhere.

Although we often hear the buzz-word 'globalisation', we are not hearing enough about those parts of the globe which actually do things differently, and most successfully. To genuinely engage in 'globalisation' means looking beyond the narrow English-speaking world. If Australia, for instance, just continues to compare its extent of inequality with the US, and to complacently recall its cultural history as being less hierarchical than Britain's, and thereby concludes

---

1   e.g. World Economic Forum, *The Global Competitiveness Report 2013–2014*, World Economic Forum, Geneva, 2013, p. 16.

that it is doing well, then this is a mere Anglo 'globalisation'. It is essential now to expand horizons, and to consider the achievements of countries such as Sweden, Finland, Denmark and Norway as public policy examples from which to learn. The English-speaking countries can benefit greatly from closer study of what the Nordic nations have accomplished with their pursuit of very different economic and social policies.

Informed analysts indicate that there is much that 'liberal market' economies in the English-speaking world can practically learn and borrow now from the success of the Nordic nations, particularly to tackle inequality.[2] The Nordic nations' emphasis upon economic equality has more potential to appeal to Australians than to the inhabitants of most other English-speaking nations. This is because Australia has traditionally had a stronger trade union movement and labour party, and a stronger ethos of being a fair and egalitarian nation, than the US, Britain and Canada.

Although the rate of trade union membership has fallen steeply in Australia over recent decades, and is very far below the clear majorities of the workforces who remain members of trade unions in all the Nordic nations, the former Right-of-centre prime minister, John Howard, discovered in his electoral defeat in 2007 that the Australian people would not accept further dismantling of industrial relations protections which are seen as bedrocks of Australian fairness. The current Right-of-centre Australian prime minister since 2013, Tony Abbott, as a result, had to solemnly pledge to not attempt the same policy changes, as a precondition for his electoral success.

---

2   e.g. Jonas Pontusson, 'Once Again a Model: Nordic Social Democracy in a
      Globalized World' in James Cronin, George Ross and James Shoch (eds.), *What's
      Left of the Left: Democrats and Social Democrats in Challenging Times*, Duke University
      Press, Durham, North Carolina, 2011, pp. 89–115.

The four main Nordic nations are still much more equal than Australia, Britain, New Zealand and Canada – and nearly twice as equal as the United States – when the disposable money income of the people in the top 10 per cent is compared with the disposable money income of the people in the bottom 10 per cent. The highest 10 per cent of income earners in Sweden, Finland, Denmark and Norway get, on average, three times what the lowest 10 per cent of income earners get. In Canada and New Zealand, the top 10 per cent of income earners get more than four times – and in Australia and Britain, the top 10 per cent get four and a half times – what the lowest 10 per cent of income earners get. In the United States, the top 10 per cent of income earners get almost six times what the lowest 10 per cent of income earners get. The Nordic nations have not been immune from the worldwide trend over recent decades towards rising inequalities. Nevertheless, in all Nordic nations, income inequalities remain dramatically lower than in English-speaking nations.[3]

A world authority on welfare, Francis G. Castles, has pointed to the industrial relations changes made by successive Australian governments from the 1990s as having thoroughly eroded the comparatively egalitarian workforce arrangements which once underpinned Australia's distinctive welfare state. He has suggested that, as a result, a positive future might require attempts to redesign Australian welfare institutions along the lines followed in parts of Europe.[4]

---

3   Figures computed from Organisation for Economic Co-operation and Development (OECD), *Divided We Stand: Why Inequality Keeps Rising*, OECD, Paris, 2011, Table A1.1 and see also p. 25 of that publication.

4   Francis G. Castles, 'Australia's Institutions and Australia's Welfare' in Geoffrey Brennan and Francis G. Castles (eds.), *Australia Reshaped: 200 Years of Institutional Transformation*, Cambridge University Press, Melbourne, 2002, p. 49.

INTRODUCTION

The Howard Government's attempt to further dismantle industrial relations protections after 2004 was partly reversed by the Labor governments of alternating prime ministers Kevin Rudd and Julia Gillard from 2007; but Australia's workforce arrangements remain far less regulated than they were in the more egalitarian period prior to the 1980s, so Castles' point stands.

The Australian Labor Party (ALP) Government from 2007 to 2013 made some positive policy achievements. This was despite its chronic leadership disunity and turnover, without which Labor may well have governed longer, as was expected when it returned to office in 2007 after having been out of government for 11 years from 1996. Most notably, Australia under Labor experienced the international economic downturn following the 2008–2009 'Global Financial Crisis' (GFC) more mildly than most countries. The unemployment rate stayed officially below 6 per cent, and Australia did not experience a technical recession, unlike nearly all other OECD nations. The Labor Government's readiness then to go into deficit and spend many billions of dollars in public funds in a timely and well-targeted way helped Australia to avoid economic downturn. The government's expansive and effective stimulus measures, starting with cash payments to individuals and households, then moving into spending on 'nation-building' projects, including for school infrastructure, together with low interest rates, helped to protect the Australian economy from, and to stave off, official recession.

However, the ALP then felt compelled to try to return the budget to surplus quickly even though this inevitably meant pain for many needy members of its own constituency and even though few market liberal economists even regarded this as necessary. The resultant spending cuts which Labor made, including to higher education and to research and development, seriously undermined its previous positive initiatives. Nor did the cuts succeed in actually returning the budget to surplus. This was because of the huge shortfall resulting from the government's failure to persevere with its Resources Super Profits Tax and to take other equitable steps to ensure adequate revenue.

The failure to entrench policy action against climate change was the Labor government's biggest failing. That failure stemmed from the then Prime Minister Rudd's decision not to break the impasse in the Australian parliament's upper house, the Senate, in early 2010 by calling a new election then on the issue. Had he done so, this would have enabled decisive action by Australia to contribute to international efforts to tackle climate change.

Since the 'Global Financial Crisis', and the continuing economic stagnation of many northen hemisphere nations on both sides of the Atlantic in its aftermath, there have also been serious problems faced by southern European nations in the Euro currency zone. This has led to much loose and generalised talk about 'Europe' as a whole being in economic crisis, as if Europe is one single entity.

Yet it is the continental northern European nation of Germany which has strongly led the developed world's re-emergence from the 'Global Financial Crisis', in contrast to Britain and the USA. The leading role taken by Germany has drawn on the strengths which it continues to have as a result of being a high-skill, coordinated and diverse economy which includes a still substantial manufacturing sector and which is not unduly reliant on risky financial speculations.[5] Sweden, Finland and Denmark all have strengths in supporting

---

5   Julian Coman, 'How Did Germany Become the New Champion of Europe?', *The Observer*, London, 2 June 2013.

export-oriented, high value-added manufacturing, including by investing very heavily in research and development, information and communications technology, and design, compared to other countries. This investment has helped them to recover well from the GFC. Sweden, as well, has many jobs in human and community services.

Nobel Prize winning economist Paul Krugman points out that, within Europe, in fact:

> the nations…in crisis *don't* have bigger welfare states than the nations doing well – if anything, the correlation runs the other way. Sweden, with its famously high benefits, is a star performer, one of the few countries whose GDP [Gross Domestic Product] is now higher than it was before the crisis. Meanwhile, before the crisis, 'social expenditure' – spending on welfare-state programs – was lower, as a percentage of national income, in *all* of the nations now in trouble than in Germany, let alone Sweden.
>
> …The euro [zone/currency] crisis, then, says nothing about the sustainability of the welfare state.[6]

While there were setbacks to the Nordic nations, including in the international economic recession of the early 1990s, and, for most, in the 2008–2009 GFC, they have continued to hold on to values such as universal welfare provision, full employment and equality. These values have helped rather than hindered these countries resume their strong overall economic, social and environmental performance since that time. There continues to be widespread public support in the Nordic nations for equality, and a strong welfare state, as consistent with economic prosperity. The resilience of these distinctive nations rebuts claims that 'globalisation' is eliminating all policy options for nation states. Among the principal reasons for their lesser increases

---

6   *New York Times*, 10 November 2011. My emphasis.

in income inequality is that the nations of Nordic Europe have continued to engage in major public social investment.[7]

The Nordic nations have also led moves to seriously cut greenhouse gas emissions in response to climate change. They were the first nations in the world to introduce carbon tax policies, doing so at the start of the 1990s. They have, in addition, heavily supported renewable energy technologies. There is much that Australia and other countries can learn from their successes in these fields.

Differences between the 'Anglo-American' countries with their 'Liberal Market Economies' (LMEs) and the continental northern European countries with their 'Co-ordinated Market Economies' (CMEs) have long been highlighted by political economists analysing 'varieties of capitalism'. Leading authors in this field argue persuasively that globalisation does not mean that all economies must become like the Anglo-American economies. Their research shows that the CMEs have consistently achieved economic progress with less inequality and shorter working hours than the LMEs, and that CMEs are more likely to support incremental innovation.[8]

Unemployment rates in Sweden, Norway and Denmark have generally been lower than in the United States, Britain, Australia and Canada.[9] From 1970 to 2000 as a whole, unemployment as a percentage of the total labour force was on average lower in Sweden and Norway than in all the English-speaking countries. Norway's unemployment rate has continued to be lower than Australia's in

---

7   Nathalie Morel, Bruno Palier and Joakim Palme's concluding chapter in their edited collection: *Towards a Social Investment Welfare State? Ideas, Policies and Challenges*, Policy Press, Bristol, 2012, pp. 356–359.

8   Peter A. Hall and David Soskice, 'Introduction' in Bob Hancké (ed.), *Debating Varieties of Capitalism: A Reader*, Oxford University Press, Oxford, 2009, pp. 37, 54.

9   Rodney Tiffen and Ross Gittins, *How Australia Compares, Second Edition*, Cambridge University Press, Melbourne, 2009, Table 4.8.

every year since 2000. Denmark's unemployment rate was higher than Australia's in only one of the 18 years from 1991 to 2008 inclusive.[10]

The landmark book first published in 2009 by British researchers Richard Wilkinson and Kate Pickett, *The Spirit Level: Why Equality is Better for Everyone*, meanwhile, powerfully shows that greater socio-economic equality of the kind which has been achieved in the Nordic nations promotes better health outcomes for all members of society.[11]

The Nokia corporation, headquartered in Espoo – Finland's second largest city after its capital city of Helsinki – rose to be, from the late 1990s until 2012, one of the world's most prominent makers of mobile phones, which were distinguished particularly by their sleek hardware design. Nokia's phones have now been eclipsed by competitors, including the Apple iPhone, which have a greater orientation to new software applications or 'apps'. Nokia's rise, nevertheless, helped to familiarise the world with Finland's success in technological innovation, remarkable for such a small country.[12] The transmission, as part of cultural globalisation, of quality political and crime television dramas from Denmark to huge audiences in English-speaking countries since the early 2000s, meanwhile, has given many people new knowledge of Danish society, culture and political processes. The surge in popularity of crime novels

---

10   OECD, *OECD Historical Statistics 1970–2000*, OECD, Paris, 2001, Table 2.14; OECD, *OECD Employment Outlook 2013*, OECD, Paris, 2013, Statistical Annex, Table A.

11   Richard Wilkinson and Kate Pickett, *The Spirit Level: Why Equality is Better for Everyone*, Penguin, London, revised paperback edition 2010.

12   On the circumstances and context of Nokia's rise, see Manuel Castells and Pekka Himanen, *The Information Society and the Welfare State: The Finnish Model*, Oxford University Press, Oxford, 2002.

from Scandinavian nations has revealed to the world some of the complexity of those nations.

The continuing visible presence of many Swedish-made Scania trucks – and Volvo buses and cars – on Australia's roads shows the rewards of the Nordic approach to competing internationally in manufacturing industry on the basis of quality products, instead of seeking to compete simply on the basis of price, with the inevitable downward pressure which this places on workers' wages. The rewards to Sweden from this industry approach are more durable than Australia's continued economic over-reliance on resource booms – driven by high demand and thus greater prices paid for mineral commodities – which have inevitably finite durations. There has been a steep decline in manufacturing in Australia, which will steepen further following the decisions made between May 2013 and February 2014 by first Ford, then General Motors (Holden) and then Toyota to cease car production in Australia altogether within a few years. Maintaining a solid manufacturing base is a long-term strength compared with becoming a country in which very few people actually make anything tangible, and given the vulnerability which economies without such a base have shown in the past. Maintaining such a base has helped Sweden, for instance, to notch up sizeable and continuous current account surpluses over the last quarter of a century, whereas massive current account deficits have been constant trends in Australia.[13]

Australia's coasting along on, and benefiting from some proceeds of, its latest resources boom was one reason why it experienced the 2008–2009 'Global Financial Crisis' more mildly than most other

13   Tiffen and Gittins, *How Australia Compares Second Edition*, Table 3.25; and OECD, *OECD Economic Outlook 2013*, OECD, Paris, 2013, Statistical Annex, Table 50.

countries. Nevertheless, while that resources boom may have helped tide Australia over, serious problems remain and will become more evident in Australia as a result of a poorly structured, unbalanced economy.

The continuing mix of strong economic performance and relatively equal income distribution in the Nordic nations makes a big and positive difference in many facets of life. There is a strong work ethos, and commitment to productivity there. At the same time, working hours remain within reasonable limits for work/life balance. In 2010, full-time workers in Australia worked on average more than three hours a week longer than workers in Finland, more than three and a half hours a week longer than workers in Sweden, more than four and a half hours longer than workers in Norway and more than five hours a week longer than workers in Denmark.[14] Updated yearly figures show that, in 2012, the average annual hours worked per person in employment were 1420 hours in Norway, 1546 hours in Denmark, 1621 hours in Sweden, 1672 hours in Finland, compared to 1728 hours in Australia.[15] The findings of a major Ipsos Mackay qualitative survey report in 2011, titled *Being Australian*, express serious concern about work intensification and excessive working hours in Australia for many now. This concern is encapsulated in one participant's statement that:

> being Australian, we want to do our eight hours a day and expect to go home to spend time with the family, our kids and that. [But] big business has made shops open longer and, even though we might be part-time, our week is stretched out a lot more

14   Barbara Pocock, Natalie Skinner, and Philippa Williams, *Time Bomb: Work, Rest and Play in Australia Today*, New South Publishing, Sydney, 2012, pp. 45, 44.

15   *OECD Employment Outlook 2013*, Statistical Annex, Table K.

because they can make the hours any time they like and we have to fit our lifestyle around it. So your whole weekend is wrecked.[16]

Many similar concerns have been expressed about the negative spillover of work demands into the family lives of Australians including because of the spread of the latest new technologies. Concerns have also been expressed about the insecurity which results from the extensively casualised employment in Australia and other English-speaking countries.[17]

In addition to keeping working hours more regulated, the Nordic nations pay attention to the working environment. Positive environments, in which workers have reasonable variety and the chance to work in teams, maximise employees' morale, commitment and output. Successful Nordic corporations, like Volvo and Scania, have been associated with innovative workplace design and a high quality of management, which involves proper consultation with – and input from – workers. Nordic nations are also more advanced than English-speaking countries in the extent to which workers' rights to participate are embedded in formal arrangements.

In discussion of specific policy problems facing Australia there is often an incidental paragraph or two, citing concrete evidence, about how much more successfully that problem is being tackled in one or more of the Nordic nations. Such references are usually to various Nordic nations' relative success in lifting children out of poverty, promoting gender equality and family-friendly workplace policies, achieving egalitarian schooling and investing in people's skills. One example is an excellent recent publication which constructively

16   Reported in *The Age*, Melbourne, and *The Sydney Morning Herald*, 25 June 2011.
17   e.g. Pocock et al, *Time Bomb*, pp. 59, 76, 177–178.

sets out policy ideas for Australia, titled *Pushing Our Luck: Ideas for Australian Progress*. Various contributors to this book mention the Nordic nations' successes in achieving well-designed public services, a comparatively high quality of private sector management, good use of resource wealth, reduction of working hours without loss of productivity and tackling climate change including through increases in renewable energy.[18]

However, following through such passing mentions of Nordic policy successes into a more in-depth study inevitably brings the objection that it is not possible to transfer programs from those nations into Australia's very different culture and institutional setup. The position of the Nordic nations is dismissed by many as culturally or historically particular.

It is obvious that the specific historic context in which the Nordic policies first came about, including the politically planned build-up of a substantial welfare state in Sweden from the 1930s to the 1970s, then the strong policy influence of feminism and children's rights from the 1970s, needs to be acknowledged. Historian Geoff Eley has described how, in Europe, 'uniquely for the Left, Scandinavian social democracy governed in the 1930s, building the welfare state's legitimacy in expansive national-popular terms', and how the ideas and influences of that period made 'social security part of Swedish national identity'. After World War II, 'the strongest parties...[continued to be] in Scandinavia, where Swedish, Norwegian and Danish socialists won repeated elections with programs of structural reform based on liberal democracy, mixed economies, trade union corporatism and

---

18   Miriam Lyons with Adrian March and Ashley Hogan (eds.), *Pushing Our Luck: Ideas for Australian Progress*, Centre for Policy Development, Sydney, 2013, pp. 30, 92, 98 n. 18, 2, 86–87, 124, 128, 137 n. 32, 139, 145 and 154 n. 31 and n. 32.

strong welfare states'. Further, 'where social democratic corporatism was strongest' such as in the Nordic nations, 'damage to the working class could be contained, whether in jobs, incomes, benefits, political representation, union organisation, the socially organised capacities of working-class communities, or the social value accorded to labour and its culture and traditions. There, even under retreat, organised labour kept better resources and self-confidence in the political arena'. Ideas for 'a revised social contract based on distributive justice, social citizenship and the welfare state...alternatives to radical marketisation...were [also] still functioning...despite the dominant neo-liberalism of the 1980s' in the Nordic nations, in contrast to many other countries.[19]

Opposition to looking further at the Nordic nations' continuing successes derives in part from the idea that national policy directions are 'path dependent'. People who emphasise 'path dependency' consider that seemingly minor decisions taken decades ago have so multiplied in importance by being enshrined into a set of patterns and routines that they are just too difficult to alter, or to contemplate following, in other nations. Yet this idea should not be pushed so far as to mean that Australia is compelled forever to chart a comparatively market liberal economic policy course, characterised by severe economic inequalities. Australia is not fated to suffer continued rates of child poverty far higher than those of Sweden, Finland, Denmark and Norway. The notion of 'path dependency' also contradicts that other widespread notion: that a tide of 'globalisation' today is so rapidly eroding all the features that used to differentiate nation states that individual countries, such as those in Nordic Europe, cannot any longer uphold their distinctive past institutions and practices.

---

19 Geoff Eley, *Forging Democracy: The History of the Left in Europe, 1850–2000*, Oxford University Press, New York, 2002, pp. 318, 314, 427, 451.

If we do accept, to some extent, the proposition that we live in more fluid and 'globalised' times today, then we cannot also accept a dogmatic proposition that our policy choices are forever frozen and predestined by paths pursued and institutions introduced many decades ago.

Centrists, moderates and social liberals tend to avoid looking to learn from Nordic nations' policies because that appears too challenging. They see the best that Australia can do is to stay or move close to the progressive end of the English-speaking family of nations, i.e. to be approximately like Canada. There are no doubt some policy lessons which Australia can learn from Canada. Some of the lessons which Australia can learn from Canada are lessons which Canada, in turn, has learned from particular Nordic nations (one example will be mentioned in Chapter 3). At the same time, Australia can learn a great deal *directly* from the Nordic nations.

Other people, nominally on the far Left, see the dramatically better real-world outcomes for the millions of people who benefit from the policy approach which is still pursued in the Nordic nations as not significant enough, in abstract theoretical, or very long-term historical, terms to warrant any action on their part. It is easy to succumb to despair at possibilities for positive change in Australia, to find excuses for neither acting nor even supporting action for better policies, claiming that it is necessary to change everything before it becomes possible to change anything. However, in fact it is not necessary for Australia's entire political culture to change before Australia adopts any of the specific positive social policy reforms which have been achieved in the Nordic nations. Steady, incremental policy changes, drawing on broader knowledge of available options from around the world, themselves help to change a country's political culture. Many people do feel genuinely overwhelmed by the large differences between the situation of Australia now and the Nordic nations. They do find it hard to identify what incremental steps Australia might take to move towards those nations' positive achievements. Hence this book will seek to identify some specific steps which can be taken – and also make better known some steps which already have been taken – in that direction.

Another general claim often made for not considering the continuing comparative income equality achievements, and the comprehensive welfare provision, of the Nordic nations as relevant is that these are simply the result of those countries being less multicultural than the English-speaking countries.

The Nordic countries are more egalitarian, it is suggested, because they are more ethnically homogeneous. People are more willing to pay taxes knowing that they are supporting people 'like themselves'. The 'multiculturalism' of English-speaking countries, however, particularly in America, is itself associated with considerable inequality and the exploitation, including segmentation in low-paid jobs, of large numbers of migrants. It has, further, never meant anything like fair treatment of the indigenous inhabitants of the nations which were colonised by Britain, nor of the African-American population.

The strong *anti*-racist record of the Nordic nations, including their leading participation in the anti-Apartheid campaigns, and their generous donation of quality aid to the world's poorer nations at levels far in excess of the pitifully low efforts of Australia and of nearly all the other English-speaking countries[20] counters the claim that their egalitarianism and generosity is linked to their comparative

---

20   Tiffen and Gittins, *How Australia Compares, Second Edition*, Table 9.4

ethnic homogeneity. Three of the four main Nordic nations have significantly higher acceptance rates of asylum seekers than Australia, with the acceptance rates in Sweden and Norway double the rate in Australia.[21]

There has also been a rise in immigration and multiculturalism *within* the Nordic nations over several decades. People who were born outside Sweden now make up more than one and a half million, or nearly 16 per cent, of Sweden's population, for instance.[22] The proportion of immigrants and their children in the Nordic nations has been growing and will continue to grow. It is certainly a valid question whether social democracy can be as strong in those countries as they become more multicultural than they used to be. Immigrants in the Nordic nations are concentrated in large numbers in particular centres like the city of Malmö in southern Sweden and in particular suburbs within cities. One of those suburbs, Husby in northern Stockholm, experienced a conflict between racial minority groups and police in May 2013, similar to conflicts which have occurred much more frequently in high immigrant cities and suburbs of Britain. Migrants in the Nordic nations, as in most developed nations, do experience lesser opportunities than local-born people. Available comparative data does indicate significantly lower employment rates of migrants in the Nordic nations than of migrants in Australia and other English-speaking countries.[23] Sweden for one needs a more effective strategy of job creation for immigrants as part of facing up to its big challenge for their more successful 'integration'. The work and

---

21   Ibid., Table 1.24.
22   Computed from data for 2013 on the Statistics Sweden website.
23   OECD, *A Profile of Immigrant Populations in the 21st Century: Data from OECD Countries*, OECD, Paris, 2008, Table 5.2.

recommendations of the Commission for a Socially Sustainable Malmö show positive signs that Sweden is doing this. There have been some limitations to what the Nordic welfare states provide for migrants and ethnic minorities. Some of these have been as a result of neo-liberal policy decisions taken, for instance, by Sweden's Reinfeldt Right-of-centre Government after its election in 2008. There is little evidence, however, that rising multiculturalism has undermined substantial welfare provision in the Nordic nations.[24]

A horrific attack took place in Norway on 22 July 2011 when an individual named Anders Breivik bombed government buildings in Oslo, killing eight people, and he then shot dead 69 young members of the Norwegian Labour Party at a camp on Utøya island, espousing xenophobic far-Right views to justify his actions. The response of the overwhelming majority of the Norwegian people, however, was to rally against Breivik's actions and to affirm that his kind of racist hatred would not prevail.

There has been in the Nordic nations, as in most other economically developed nations since the late 1990s, some electoral backlash to rising immigration and multiculturalism. The return in Denmark in September 2011 of a government led by the Social Democrats, with Helle Thorning-Schmidt as the nation's first female prime minister, ended a decade of Liberal-Conservative rule. The Social Democrat-led government has rescinded some of the very hostile actions against immigrants and asylum-seekers introduced by the Right-of-centre government which preceded it. The Danish Social Democrats went to the 2011 election with promises to raise taxes on banks and the

---

24   Stephen Castles and Carl-Ulrik Schierup, 'Migration and Ethnic Minorities' in Francis G. Castles, Stephan Leibfried, Jane Lewis, Herbert Obinger and Christopher Pierson (eds.), *The Oxford Handbook of the Welfare State*, Oxford University Press, Oxford, paperback edition 2012, pp. 278–291.

wealthy to help pay for better schools and hospitals. It also pledged to spend substantially more on welfare.

Departures from traditional economic policies by mainstream Left-of-centre parties when in office since the 1980s have contributed to the fragmentation of their voting support, including a rise in support for xenophobic far-Right 'populist' parties, particularly among blue-collar voters. These trends have been connected with the uptake of policies hostile to immigrants and refugees by the established Right, to the electoral detriment of the mainstream Left. Declines in votes for the long-standing major parties on the Left of centre (labour, social democratic or socialist) have occurred steadily in recent decades in many countries. Frequently, however, this decline has occurred within a continuing electoral majority – or close to it – for Left-of-centre parties overall, leading to formation of coalitions between them. Labour and social democratic parties can expect support to return to them as economic policy questions become more central again for voters. This support will return when clearer differences between the labour and social democratic parties on the one hand, and Right-of-centre parties on the other hand, in their answers to those questions are articulated.

The Swedish Social Democratic Party has enjoyed unparalleled electoral – and enduring policy – success over its history. The Danish Social Democrats and the Norwegian Labour Party have been almost as successful. In Finland, the Social Democratic Party has not been as electorally successful but it has had considerable influence, particularly on education policy over recent decades. These parties have had their own serious setbacks since their golden periods. This includes the Swedish Social Democratic Party being out of office for two terms from 2006 to 2014. However, even then its opponents had to concede much policy ground to beat the Swedish Social Democrats; which shows how Left-of-centre parties can, with clear ideas and purpose, set the terms of policy in developed nations. In so far as they have neo-liberalised less than the Anglo-Australasian labour parties (i.e. the British, Australian and New Zealand labour parties), the details of the Nordic social democratic parties' lasting policy achievements are of immense value for social democrats in the English-speaking world to study afresh. Such study can help to identify policy goals which those people can now aim for; and which the Anglo-Australasian labour parties can now rebuild towards achieving.

No party other than the Social Democrats has governed for more than two consecutive terms in Sweden since 1932. Even in Sweden's 2006 and 2010 elections, when the Social Democratic Party was defeated, voters did not reject the fundamentals of the welfare state.[25] Nor did the Swedish people in those elections vote in favour of more inequality on the scale that it exists in the English-speaking world. A majority of people in the Nordic nations evidently want to preserve social democratic policy achievements for the future. Now that it has been re-elected to government in September 2014, the Swedish Social Democratic Party, like the social democratic parties and trade union movements in all of the Nordic nations, is looking at how to act most effectively to preserve and to adapt those achievements for the future. The directions which they take will be of great relevance to Australia, and so are the positions from which they start.

---

25   Stefan Svallfors, 'Public Attitudes' in Francis G. Castles et al (eds.), *The Oxford Handbook of the Welfare State*, pp. 241–251.

The Scope and Structure of this Book

This book spans several disciplines, including history, social policy, public health, education and economics. It uses several techniques – including original archival research; selection, presentation and interpretation of data; and interactions and interviews with policy actors – to add to understandings of what can be learned by Australia, and other English-speaking countries, from the policy achievements of the three principal Scandinavian countries and Finland.

Previous outside policy interest in the Nordic nations is surveyed in Chapter 1. The book then shows, in the subsequent chapters, policy lessons in some vital areas which Australia can now learn from the achievements of Sweden, Finland, Denmark and Norway. The focusing of each of those chapters on one of the four main Nordic nations, and on one particular policy area for each, is not intended to imply that the same, or a similar, policy is not followed in the other three main Nordic nations. The intention, instead, is to illustrate a particular policy *strength* of each nation. Many additional policy areas could also be chosen, but that would mean a much bigger book.

Perhaps most importantly of all, the Nordic nations are notable for driving child poverty down to unparalleled lows, to about half the rate which prevails in Australia. This achievement is connected with the Nordic nations' high levels of gender equality, their high female and general labour force participation rates and their provision of family-friendly workplace arrangements. Those arrangements include, in Sweden, sixteen months' paid parental leave, a minimum of two months of which must be taken by fathers. **Sweden's leading role in reducing child poverty, and improving children's wellbeing, is explored in Chapter 2.**

Many believed that the successes of Scandinavian style social democracy were well-placed to guide the former Communist countries following the demise of the Soviet Union and the collapse of authoritarian rule in Eastern Europe in the early 1990s. Instead, free market shock therapy was applied in the former Soviet Union and Eastern Europe. The consequence has been a backlash from many people in those countries against the massive rises of inequality, and loss of security and material benefits, which the changeover to capitalism has meant. There has also been a scandalous failure to win democracy in many of those countries. Finland, however, stands as a stark regional contrast. Finland is a direct neighbour of Russia, whereas the Scandinavian nations are not, and the Finnish language is very different from the Scandinavian languages of Swedish, Danish and Norwegian. Finland was deeply, negatively disrupted by the fall of the Soviet Union with which it had been so economically entangled, and by the simultaneous 1990s global recession. From that time, however, Finland pursued a positive, social democratic Scandinavian strategy, rather than the approach which has led to the disgrace that is Vladimir Putin's Russia today. This contributed to Finland's success in information technology innovation. Finland's experience is thus generally informative about the possibilities for nation states to make changes in policy direction. Finland is also specifically informative about how Australia should seek to meet the huge challenges which it now faces to achieve both higher quality in, and greater equality between, schools. These challenges exist because of a long-term failure to fund government schools in Australia adequately, as identified in Australia's Gonski report, which makes important recommendations for change. In Finland, also, vocational education is not regarded as culturally inferior to general academic learning, and it includes high general education skills. **Finland's stunning success in schools, which has been evident since the 1990s, will be examined in Chapter 3.**

One reason for the Nordic nations' long-standing low levels of unemployment is their policy commitment to ensuring adequate support and job skills training for those who do become unemployed. English-speaking countries can learn from the particular success of Denmark's comprehensive, activating labour programs in assisting unemployed people. Denmark emphasises *employment* security. This is different from *job* security i.e. security in one particular job. Employment security involves extensive skills training support for adaptation and transition into new jobs for adults who are affected by changes to their old job. **Denmark's commitment to skills enhancement and its endeavour to combine security with flexibility in employment – sometimes referred to as 'Flexicurity' – are explored in Chapter 4.**

In three of the four main Nordic nations – Sweden, Finland and Denmark – manufacturing makes up a large share of the economy. Norway's economy, by contrast, is like Australia's in that it relies much more on resources.[26] However, unlike Australia, Norway uses its present resource riches wisely, building up financial reserves for the years after the resources inevitably run out. Norway thus aims to sustain its national inheritance. Concern about Australia being a quarry, taking non-renewable resources out of the ground to benefit from short-term booms in demand for those resources – rather than building a range of more durable foundations for economic prosperity – persists. The contrast with Norway in this respect is stark. In

---

26   e.g. Tiffen and Gittins, *How Australia Compares, Second Edition*, Table 3.20.

Australia to date, the benefits from resources booms have largely been wasted by not adequately taxing the huge profits, which have gone, as a result, to a very wealthy few, further exacerbating economic inequalities. **The Norwegian approach to ensuring that the whole nation benefits in the long term from its natural resource wealth will be examined in Chapter 5.** That approach has implications for Australia's pressing need to face up to the stark arithmetic reality that it must now fairly raise more general taxation revenue if it is to fund necessary increases in public health, education, transport and infrastructure services and to take more serious environmental initiatives to respond to climate change.

Chapter 1

PREVIOUS POLICY INTEREST IN THE NORDIC NATIONS

An intermittent interest by some people from English-speaking nations in the policy achievements of the Nordic nations began soon after the breakthrough election victory by the Social Democratic Party (SAP) to form government in Sweden in 1932. At this election, the party gained clear support for its radical economic program to tackle the Great Depression. After that election, the SAP was continuously re-elected so that it governed for 44 consecutive years.

In 1936 an American journalist, Marquis Childs, published a book titled *Sweden: The Middle Way*. Childs's book became a bestseller and went into many reprints and editions. Childs had been impressed, during visits to Sweden in the 1930s, by the energy and scope of Swedish initiatives to reduce unemployment and to tackle the economic depression which bedevilled the world in that decade. He identified their basis in comprehensive revenue collection and astute expenditure. Childs was also attracted by the practical approach taken by consumer co-operatives to bring down prices, the methodical mobilisation of public support to this end and the application of co-operative methods to provide quality low-cost housing and furnishings, particularly for families with children. In addition, he praised the pragmatic and efficient Swedish approach to industry development, generous but prudently planned aged pension arrangements, widespread participation in organisations including the trade unions, and brilliance of art and design. He also praised what he saw as the general sense of 'moderation' and social cohesion and the way 'the Social Democrats... [were] committed to a cautious gradualism, advancing step by step with the approval of the overwhelming mass of the voters'. Childs included a chapter on Denmark as well, mentioning how its 'socialised education has produced advanced social laws, pertaining to women and children, public health, [and] the hours and conditions of labour'.[1]

The British Fabian Society also noticed the achievements of the Social Democratic Party governments of Sweden in the 1930s. One of the Society's leading members, Margaret Cole, led a delegation to Sweden, which resulted in a set of essays published by the New Fabian Research Bureau in 1938.[2]

There was a notable early episode of interest in Swedish social democratic policy achievements too by Australian Keynesian economist and leading public servant H.C. 'Nugget' Coombs. In the late 1930s, Coombs studied the policy which Sweden had pursued to recover from economic depression. In 1946 he visited Sweden on behalf of Australia's Labor Government as part of discussions on international financial arrangements, during which he forged a good rapport with leading Swedish economist Gunnar Myrdal, who was then Minister for Trade in Sweden's Social Democratic Government.[3]

---

1   Marquis W. Childs, *Sweden: The Middle Way*, Yale University Press, New Haven, Connecticut, 1936, pp. 164, 142.

2   Margaret Cole and Charles Smith (eds.), *Democratic Sweden: A Volume of Studies Prepared by Members of the New Fabian Research Bureau*, Books for Libraries Press, New York, 1970, reprint (first published by Routledge, London, 1938).

3   Tim Rowse, *Nugget Coombs: A Reforming Life*, Cambridge University Press, Melbourne, 2005, pp. 87–90, 130, 186.

Interest in Sweden then evidently developed in the Australian trade union movement during the 1960s, from which time two politically different parts of the movement – first the Right, then the Left – made contacts. There were distinctive features of the Left-wing Australian unionists' turn towards Sweden. They were especially interested in industrial democracy and work design as a result of links which had been forged between particular Swedish, Norwegian and Australian academics, labour movement intellectuals and activists from the late 1960s.

A central person in these interactions was Olle Hammarström, who joined the Swedish Social Democratic Party while studying for a master's degree at Gothenburg in 1967. Involvement with the Sociology Department there led him into an international network, prominent in which was an Australian named Fred Emery, who had been based at the Tavistock Institute of Human Relations in London since the late 1950s. Emery, along with colleagues, developed 'socio-technical' ideas about the value of enabling employees to have more control over their work environment. Emery was particularly associated with the idea of a 'search conference' as the method and starting-point for bringing together people in different parts of a company to talk about issues and prospects, then move into autonomous work groups.[4]

Norway's small scale and relative cohesion led to it being deemed the most suitable country to try out these alternative ideas of work organisation. 'Industrial Democracy' was included as a bargaining item in the basic agreements between unions and employers in Norway from the early 1960s. Emery, and the Work Research Institute

---

4   Interview with Olle Hammarström.

created in Oslo in the 1970s to examine issues in workplace reform, led the trialling of autonomous work groups in Norway. Several Norwegian unionists and academics became part of this movement to change the labour process in a way which would make work more fulfilling for workers.

The ideas were then carried to Sweden, where they were widely and rapidly diffused. Olle Hammarström became a researcher and activist during this wave of industrial democracy experiments in Sweden in the early 1970s. He then went to work in Sweden's Ministry of Labour from 1974 to 1978 as a policy adviser on industrial democracy and the work environment. In this capacity he received many Australian government and union visitors, including shipbuilding delegates in 1974, who visited the then state-owned shipyards in Uddevalla, 90 kilometres from Gothenburg. These delegations also made contact with the Swedish Metal Workers' Union.[5]

A former union leader, Clyde Cameron, became Australia's minister for workplace matters when Gough Whitlam led the Australian Labor Party into government in 1972. Cameron was interested in the ideas of younger industrial relations scholars in Australia who had union sympathies, and they became important sources of knowledge for him. One of these was G. W. (Bill) Ford, who drew Cameron's attention to initiatives in Sweden for reform of working life. Bill Ford was an early school-leaver from a blue-collar family who returned to study. By 1971 he was an academic at the University of New South Wales, with a strong interest in different approaches to work organisation and 'skill formation' (a term he preferred to 'training', because 'training' implies merely imparting one person's knowledge

---

5   Correspondence file relating to Australia in the records of the Swedish Metal Workers' Union (IF Metall), Stockholm, for the year 1974.

into another). He had begun to hear of developments in this field in Sweden, including the work of Gösta Rehn on active labour market policies. Gösta Rehn and Rudolf Meidner were economists at Sweden's confederation of trade unions who formulated the wages solidarity policy, which was pursued with great economic success in Sweden from the 1950s to the 1970s. Bill Ford became engrossed in finding out more about Swedish union research, education and initiatives for industrial democracy. This entailed much work (which he would continue for decades) in obtaining a wider range of materials than was then available in Australia. Ford sent Clyde Cameron materials about these matters, which he put to use.[6]

In 1972 Clyde Cameron attended an address given in Melbourne by Pehr Gyllenhammar, President of Sweden's Volvo group of companies, and then spoke positively about his message:

> Mr Gyllenhammar...typifies the new breed of young executives that is taking over the control of the world's most progressive enterprises...[He] advocated a closer relationship between management and labour...[including] appointment of employees' representatives to boards of management,...steps that will produce job satisfaction by the introduction of group production in place of the soul-destroying monotony of the assembly line; and said that there must be a long-term solution that will make people want to work without threats.[7]

Cameron quoted a statement by a leading Swedish trade union leader that:

> growing numbers of people expect increasingly more of the environment in which they work. They want the physical and

---

6   Interview with Bill Ford.
7   Clyde Cameron, 'Modern Technology, Job Enrichment and the Quality of Life', *Journal of Industrial Relations*, Vol. 14, No. 4, December 1972, p. 368.

mental strains of their work reduced. They want their jobs to be diversified, made interesting, given meaning. People are demanding greater autonomy, more say in how they carry out their jobs. They [also] want to...[make] jobs secure for the future.[8]

As Minister for Labour following Whitlam's election in December 1972, Cameron appointed Bill Ford to his staff as a special adviser. Ford then accompanied Cameron on an official overseas mission from May 1973 (which was Ford's first visit to Sweden). Ford was with Cameron when he and his Swedish ministerial counterpart signed a program for exchange of industrial democracy personnel between the two countries.

The influence of the 1973 Swedish visit and of Bill Ford's ideas are evident in several speeches which Cameron gave to audiences of managers following his return. He cited the examples of leading Swedish companies, such as Volvo, in pioneering industrial democracy. He issued a challenge to the managers of Australian firms 'to drag...your directors out of the backwaters into which they have allowed their companies to drift' and 'to follow the pragmatists of Europe'.[9]

Cameron referred to Emery's criticism of the way work had become more boring, workers had become more controlled, the identity formerly provided by a worker's craft had become endangered and loyalty to a particular job or organisation had lessened during movement through a succession of similar, low-level jobs. Further, he expressed concerns that control over machinery and jobs had passed to managers and designers, while workers' needs for self-actualisation

---

8   Ibid. pp. 370–371.

9   Clyde Cameron, *Managerial Control and Industrial Democracy, Myths and Realities: An Address*, Australian Government Publishing Service, Canberra, 1973, pp. 9, 11.

had been diminished. Consequently, he said, there was a need for 'job enrichment…to make work once more a meaningful, satisfying activity…by placing an emphasis on team building'. Again he referred to Gyllenhammar's company:

> probably the most well-known series of experiments carried out over the last ten years are those undertaken at the Volvo Corporation, Sweden…[which is] convinced that human beings have an intrinsic need to work in groups, to feel that they belong to a team, to be shown appreciation for a job they are doing well…and…[to] identify themselves positively with the product they are helping to produce.[10]

Bill Ford recalls how he and Cameron visited magnificently appointed union colleges on the banks of fjords and believes that it was these experiences in Sweden which assured the formation of Australia's Trade Union Training Authority by the Whitlam Government.[11]

The international public service exchange of personnel between Sweden and Australia went ahead despite the sudden fall of the Whitlam Government in November 1975. As part of this, an Australian public servant spent 15 months in Sweden from October 1975 to January 1977, resulting in a book.[12] In return, Olle Hammarström, together with his wife and close colleague Ruth Hammarström, spent 15 months in Australia from August 1976 to late 1977. After initially being located at the Melbourne head office of Australia's Department of Employment and Industrial Relations, it was agreed that Olle

---

10 Clyde Cameron, *Human Satisfaction, Current Social Standards and Their Effect on Work, Production and Productivity: Address*, Australian Government Publishing Service, Canberra, 1974, pp. 4, 5, 6, 10.

11 Ford interview. See also Bill Guy, *A Life on the Left: A Biography of Clyde Cameron*, Wakefield Press, Adelaide, 1999, pp. 273, 307, 360–361.

12 Doron Gunzburg, *Industrial Democracy Approaches in Sweden: An Australian View*, Productivity Promotion Council of Australia, Melbourne, 1978.

Hammarström could be based in the Department's Adelaide branch office.

The reason the Hammarströms wanted to go to Adelaide was because an Industrial Democracy Unit had been formed by the South Australian State Government in 1974. This was the result of Labor Premier Don Dunstan's interest, which was enhanced by his own visit to Sweden and meeting with Swedish Social Democratic Prime Minister Olof Palme in that year.[13] Officials of the new Unit, influenced by Emery's ideas, had visited Sweden and met with Olle Hammarström there in his role in the Ministry of Labour. They had also visited the new Volvo factory in Kalmar, Sweden.[14]

Ruth Hammarström joined this South Australian Unit for Industrial Democracy, co-wrote two of its papers with Olle Hammarström on Sweden and jointly authored another on women and industrial democracy.[15] The Hammarströms emphasised that industrial democracy in Sweden meant more than individual cases like Volvo, important though they were. The Hammarströms argued that it was the breadth of development of industrial democracy in Sweden, its strong popular support and comprehensive structural underpinnings which made Sweden's experience especially noteworthy.[16] The Hammarströms formed close contacts with many Australian industrial relations academics and practitioners in 1976

---

13   Don Dunstan, *Felicia: The Political Memoirs of Don Dunstan*, Macmillan, Melbourne, 1981, pp. 227, 230.

14   Files for June and August 1974 in the records of the Swedish Metal Workers' Union, Stockholm.

15   Ruth Hammarström and Olle Hammarström, *Industrial Democracy in Sweden, Parts 1 and 2*, Unit for Industrial Democracy, Premier's Department, Adelaide, 1977; Susan Walpole and Ruth Hammarström, *Women and Industrial Democracy*, Unit for Industrial Democracy, Premier's Department, Adelaide, 1977.

16   Hammarström and Hammarström, *Industrial Democracy in Sweden, Part 1*, p. 22.

and 1977, which continued afterwards. The Hammarströms then returned to Sweden, and Olle Hammarström became Research Director in 1978 of the recently formed Swedish Centre for Working Life. This Centre became an important base for many visiting Australian academics, including Winton Higgins (about whom more below) and Geoff Dow, a Queensland political economy academic.

South Australian Premier Don Dunstan held a major international conference on industrial democracy in Adelaide in 1978. The most prominent places were given to speakers from Norway and Sweden. Approximately 400 delegates from companies, unions and government departments attended, and a comprehensive 700-page edited volume of proceedings was professionally published.[17]

Fred Emery and Bill Ford (who advocated forming a Work Research Institute as Norway had recently done) were among the speakers at this conference.[18] In his contribution, Dunstan expressed similar sentiments to Clyde Cameron about the importance of greater democracy at work, including for its economic benefits. In his opening address he said that:

> there are those who believe that giving employees any real involvement in their organisation will lead to a decrease in efficiency. I cannot accept this viewpoint especially in the light of the economic success of such countries as…Sweden.[19]

In discussion with conference participants, Dunstan emphasised that 'the question of job satisfaction is at the root of the matter'.[20] Some contributors to the conference argued for industrial democracy on

---

17 Ray Wood (ed.), *Proceedings of the International Conference on Industrial Democracy, Adelaide, South Australia*, CCH Australia, Sydney, 1978.

18 Ibid. pp. 653–657.

19 Dunstan, 'Opening Address' ibid. p. 4.

20 Ibid. p. 15.

the grounds that it was not radical, stating that it 'has only been able to gather the momentum that it has because of the combination of social, technological and educational forces which have forced... [it] into prominence in most countries in the western industrialised world'.[21]

This portrayal of industrial democracy in the Nordic nations as not radical fitted with the long-standing view of Swedish social democracy as a pragmatic 'middle way'. That view was mirrored in the French socialist François Mitterrand's complaint, following the SAP's 1976 election defeat after 44 continuous years in office, that Sweden's Social Democrats had not pursued more radical measures, such as the nationalisation of large industries.[22]

In 1977, Bob Carr, the future Labor Premier of New South Wales (from 1995 to 2005) and Foreign Minister of Australia (from 2012 to 2013), always on the Right of the ALP, similarly upheld Swedish social democracy as a respectable and successful alternative to what he characterised as the more ideologically simplistic position of the British and Australian labour parties.[23] Looking to the 'Swedish model' came to be associated with Tony Crosland and the moderate Right of the British Labour Party from the 1950s.

Other observers of Sweden, however, took a different view, arguing that Swedish achievements were in fact radical. For example, in 1978, Francis G. Castles, a British scholar of Scandinavian social democracy, and of comparative public policy – prior to his moving to

21   Ibid. p. 21.
22   Cited in Francis G. Castles, *The Social Democratic Image of Society: A Study of the Achievements and Origins of Scandinavian Social Democracy in Comparative Perspective*, Routledge and Kegan Paul, London, 1978, p. 3.
23   Bob Carr, *Social Democracy and Australian Labor*, NSW Labor Day Committee, Sydney, 1977, pp. 7–8, 20, 22.

Australia and becoming a world authority on welfare – challenged the perception that Swedish social democracy was merely moderate and middle-of-the road. Castles criticised Crosland for not acknowledging the extent to which the success of Scandinavian social democratic parties in winning elections and implementing their policies was actually the result of their emphasis on being parties of, and for, the working class. He further criticised Crosland for not recognising those parties' achievement in creating a clear egalitarian and welfare-orientated social democracy as the prevailing image of their societies, in contrast to the economic individualism which continued to prevail as the dominant national ethos of Britain.[24]

Also in 1978, Swedish sociologist Walter Korpi argued that it was the 'historical compromise' which Sweden's comparatively strong labour movement had been able to impose on employers which explained the SAP's policy successes.[25] Then, in 1979, an American sociologist, John D. Stephens, argued that Swedish social democracy had actually reformed society so radically that Sweden should rightly now be regarded as being close to a socialist country.[26] Meanwhile, from the mid-1970s, observers from the resurgent free-market Right joined the debate about Sweden's 'middle way'. They put the 'Swedish model' 'on trial' for its insistence on equality, high levels of taxation and universal welfare provision. Hence, in 1980, Marquis Childs published a sequel to his 1936 volume, titled *Sweden: The Middle Way on Trial*.[27]

---

24 Castles, *The Social Democratic Image of Society*, 1978, pp. 97, 119, 125, 127, 131, 141.

25 Walter Korpi, *The Working Class in Welfare Capitalism: Work, Unions and Politics in Sweden*, Routledge and Kegan Paul, London, 1978, pp. 320–321.

26 John D. Stephens, *The Transition from Capitalism to Socialism*, Macmillan, London, 1979.

27 Marquis W. Childs, *Sweden: The Middle Way on Trial*, Yale University Press, New Haven, Connecticut, 1980.

By the early 1980s, support for and interest in Sweden came to be more associated with the Left of academia and the labour movement than with the Right of the labour movement and politics as before. Increased interest in Sweden had been developing among the Left from the mid-1970s in many English-speaking countries, including in the United States, Canada and Britain. This followed the assertive moves by Swedish trade unions to establish wage-earner funds, into which it was proposed that a very substantial proportion of private sector profits should be placed to create very large union-run accumulations of capital, in a radical attempt to spread economic ownership more collectively. These moves indicated that the Swedish labour movement was challenging free-market capitalism more fundamentally than previous depictions of it as merely pragmatic and reformist would have led many people to expect.

In Australia the Left unions, by the 1980s, were seeking new ways ahead from their tradition of organising under non-Labor governments during a long period of prosperity which had ended. Nordic models, for a time, would replace various earlier international influences on the Australian Left from places including Britain.

The national leadership of Australia's major Left-wing union, the Amalgamated Metal Workers' Union (AMWU),[28] kept itself at some distance from the 1970s South Australian industrial democracy initiatives. Its formal policy, adopted in 1974, strongly opposed notions of 'worker participation' and 'job enrichment',[29] out of suspicion that such ideas replaced correct notions of class conflict with class collaboration, and would lead to workers becoming incorporated into

---

28   Now the Australian Manufacturing Workers' Union.
29   Nick Ruskin, 'Union Policy on Industrial Democracy: The Case of the AMWU' in Ed Davis and Russell Lansbury (eds.), *Democracy and Control in the Workplace*, Longmans, Melbourne, 1986. pp. 180, 182.

company perspectives instead of acting as independent unionists. The Union expressed this position at the 1978 Adelaide conference.[30] Others at that conference, however, saw radical potential in industrial democracy. And the AMWU would soon considerably develop its own ideas for a radical notion of industrial democracy, with the ambition of assertively intervening in 'managerial prerogative', which led it, in turn, towards interest in the Nordic nations.[31]

In order to become more informed for the debate which was emerging in Australia about industrial democracy, researchers within the AMWU had made broad international enquiries during 1973. They gathered several publications about worker participation in management from Swedish unions and governmental bodies. They also obtained materials from unions in Norway and Denmark, including an outline of the Danish unions' agenda then for 'economic democracy'.[32] An article from overseas about 'the Volvo Experiment' appeared in a 1973 AMWU publication. It described the initiatives as a:

> revolutionary retreat from the orthodox assembly-line technique…laid down by Henry Ford…[following] a long-standing and persistent search by the Swedish autoworkers themselves for greater variation in their jobs [and] a deep desire… to perform more meaningful tasks in the plant [through] further training and development of skills.

These new measures included movement between a variety of positions in an enterprise so that:

---

30 Wood (ed.), *Proceedings of the International Conference on Industrial Democracy*, pp. 256–261.

31 Discussed in Ruskin's 'Union Policy on Industrial Democracy', pp. 176–191.

32 AMWU records in the Australian National University's Noel Butlin Archives Centre, Deposit Z102, Box 268 ('Industrial Democracy 1950–1980').

workers deepen their knowledge of the operations as a whole by learning several jobs…'job-widening'…[which brings greater] experience in the operations as a whole and greater job satisfaction from team work with their fellow-workers on the line…consultative meetings…proposals…for complete reorganisation of the work area in the factory…[and] at Volvo-Kalmar…as planned now, the assembly of car bodies will be divided among a number of working teams.[33]

Multiple copies of this article were made for wider distribution in the union. All of these materials give indications of being closely read, with underlinings, annotations and pages of handwritten notes being made. From the mid-to-late 1970s, AMWU officers made contact with their Swedish counterparts to request any further information in English that could be provided; and they visited Sweden to look at trade union education establishments, techniques and programs, where they were impressed by the widespread debate underway among workers over the radical proposal for wage-earner funds.[34]

As Australian union interest in Sweden extended to more influential labour movement leaders in the 1980s, the most important of these was Laurie Carmichael. Carmichael was a leading Metal Workers' Union official who made his first visit to Sweden in 1971 to attend the Stockholm Conference on the Vietnam War. The AMWU had actively opposed America's involvement in Vietnam from the war's inception in 1964. Sweden's Social Democratic Party Government under Olof Palme was more critical of American involvement in Vietnam than any other government in the Western world.

A dynamic, militant and effective national union leader, Carmichael had represented workers in the car industry for many years,

---

33   Amalgamated Metal Unions, *Monthly Journal*, Sydney, April 1973, pp. 11–13.
34   See further: Andrew Scott, 'Looking to Sweden in order to Reconstruct Australia', *Scandinavian Journal of History*, Vol. 34, No. 3, September 2009, pp. 330–352.

which had led him to explore issues about work organisation in a Marxian framework. He had a longstanding passion to create more opportunities for workers to advance their skills. He also had a strong interest in the implications of new technology and extensive international contacts.

Carmichael's growing disaffection with official Communism, especially after the Soviet suppression of the Prague Spring in 1968, led him to look towards alternative political approaches from that time, which led gradually to an interest in industrial democracy. As a result, the AMWU developed close links with the Swedish Metal Workers' Union from the 1970s and then an intense interest in Sweden during the 1980s. Carmichael's search became more urgent in the early 1980s following his own ambivalence about the success of the recent campaign, in which he had been central, for higher wages and shorter working hours in the Australian manufacturing industry. Carmichael later considered that this campaign would have been better directed at gaining paid study leave, as the Scandinavian metal unions had done.[35]

A new Australian Labor Government was elected in 1983 under Prime Minister Bob Hawke. A Prices and Incomes Accord was negotiated between the Australian Council of Trade Unions (ACTU) and the new Australian Labor Government as part of seeking a more effective and sophisticated strategy for the labour movement in those challenging economic times. This committed unions to wages restraint in exchange for government measures for price control, 'social wage' provision, industrial democracy and industry policy.

Crucially, the leadership of the AMWU was willing, by 1983, to actively support this Prices and Incomes Accord. While the Accord

---

35   Interview with Laurie Carmichael.

formally survived for the whole life of the Labor Government (1983–1996), it was widely felt from the early years that the Government was failing to fulfil most of its policy obligations. Debates developed during the 1980s on whether or not the Left unions should continue with the Accord, following disappointments with the Hawke Government's deregulatory economic policies and limited action on industry policy. The experience of Sweden, one of few other countries besides Australia in which a labour, social democratic or socialist party was then in office, became very important in those debates.

The inability of other Left-of-centre parties that were in government from the early 1980s, including (by then) Mitterrand in France and Hawke in Australia, to follow through with the expansionary economic policies in their original platforms indicated how much the Swedish Social Democratic Party had actually achieved in preceding decades. This point was reinforced by the SAP's return to office in 1982 (albeit with a modified program), and the comparatively low unemployment rates which that government maintained in Sweden throughout the 1980s. In 1985, the British Fabian Society renewed its own interest in Sweden, publishing a pamphlet by a journalist aligned with the Labour Party positively analysing *The Swedish Road to Socialism*.[36]

By 1985, Laurie Carmichael, after visiting Sweden again, became so enthused by the unions' achievements in that country that he acted on the basis of them to shape the direction of Australian industrial relations differently than otherwise would have been the case. Carmichael and many colleagues found inspiration in the achievements of Swedish trade unions and social democracy. This led them

36   Martin Linton, *The Swedish Road to Socialism*, Fabian Society, London, 1985.

to try to transform and transcend a defensive local labourism and to push for alternative, more ambitious political strategies than the dominant neo-liberalised Labor Right in Australia would consider.

Carmichael was aware of the strong employer opposition in Sweden to wage-earner funds as a result of his international visits, and this contributed towards his increased political interest in Sweden by the mid-1980s. The Olof Palme Government's eventual introduction in 1983 of a modified form of wage-earner funds was much more limited than the original concept developed by the Swedish trade union movement in the 1970s, but it was still impressive to overseas visitors. Carmichael was a national research officer of the AMWU from late 1984 until he was elected assistant national secretary of the ACTU in July 1987. In the period 1984–1987, Carmichael helped to maintain the Left unions' support for the Accord, while at the same time lobbying inside the ACTU for policy change. He also made occasional, strong public criticism of the Labor Government's failure to honour central commitments of the Accord.

Winton Higgins was another Australian who had met the Hammarströms in 1976–1977. Higgins had previously spent a year in Sweden in 1969–1970, and then, after becoming an academic at Macquarie University in Sydney in 1976, he returned to Sweden in 1979 in a period of study leave. He stayed with a local family there, built up his language skills to become fluent in the Swedish language and knowledgeable about the achievements of the Swedish trade union movement; and he became increasingly intrigued by what that movement had achieved. He was based at Stockholm's Institute for Social Research.[37]

---

37   Interview with Winton Higgins.

In 1979 Higgins published an article which began with the words: 'It takes a good deal of courage to write, for an Anglo-Saxon audience, an article claiming that socialism is developing in Sweden'.[38] This article circulated in an influential way in the AMWU. Higgins' contention that socialism was developing in Sweden was based partly on the ability of the Swedish trade union confederation, the *Landsorganisationen* (LO), since the 1950s, to influence the SAP to adopt radical policies, such as the Co-determination Act of 1976 to promote industrial democracy. It was based also on LO's proposals for wage-earner funds. Higgins commented that: 'LO…is much more than a… union confederation comparable with…the ACTU in Australia. It has developed a practice of national policy formation and implementation outside the framework of the state, and thus is also partly extra-parliamentary party and partly alternative state apparatus'.[39]

Another important person in this coalescing network was Ted Wilshire, a former metal worker who went to study political economy at Sydney University. He was then appointed in 1976 at Laurie Carmichael's initiative as an AMWU researcher. The AMWU had links with the Sydney-based political economy movement in its phase of exposing and criticising the growing power of transnational corporations. Wilshire's energetic education campaigns in the AMWU were positively reported in one of that movement's publications.[40] In 1981, Wilshire took leave from the AMWU to work for Lionel Bowen, Deputy ALP Leader. When the Hawke Labor Government was elected in 1983, Wilshire became executive

38   Winton Higgins, 'Working Class Mobilisation and Socialism in Sweden', *Intervention*, No. 13, October 1979, pp. 5–18.
39   Ibid. p. 17.
40   Greg Crough and Ted Wheelwright, *Australia: A Client State*, Penguin, Melbourne, 1982, p. 210.

director of a Unit later named the Trade Development Council, inside the Department of Trade for which Bowen was the new minister.

Winton Higgins published a new academic journal article in August 1985, which was reprinted in a way that increased its circulation and impact and which had a marked influence on Carmichael. This article built on Higgins' earlier writings and emphasised how 'the Swedish labour-market reforms of the 1970s...substantially increased the powers...of union workplace organisations', and identified 'recessions...[and] longer term investment behaviour that winds down industrial activity' as 'attacks on working and living conditions...which...cannot be turned back by the strike weapon'. He argued strongly against elements in the Left who simplistically dismissed Accord-type arrangements and who 'interpret...any union concern for anti-recessionary politics...as class collaboration'. Higgins contended that 'a developing political unionism...must develop central...co-ordinating...leaderships, which in turn must arm themselves with an ever-expanding body of knowledge...to match the resources and discipline of their adversaries'.

Further, as 'the union movement...projects itself into more and more policy areas, its social monitoring and constant policy initiatives necessitate permanent in-house research establishments', Higgins argued. He outlined the great political achievements which Swedish unions had made through their industry-wide bargaining, including for the lowest paid, and the Swedish labour movement's long-standing recognition that 'wage levels...depend ultimately on industrial performance, which now must become a union concern'. He contended therefore that 'the movement's "production policy"', though 'often...cited as evidence of Swedish unionism's deep commitment to class collaboration...[actually] had its immediate theoretical antecedents in the party theoretician Ernst Wigforss' critique from 1919 of capitalism's...chronic disorganisation...as inseparably linked to its perverse distribution of income and mass unemployment'. Higgins also emphasised that Sweden's 'Rehn-Meidner model...gives the union movement a central role in policy formation'. Whereas earlier Australian observers had interpreted scarcity of strikes in Sweden as a sign of enlightened management, Higgins argued that they were actually the product of the unions' strategic strength.[41]

Winton Higgins was invited to participate in AMWU training schools during this period. His scholarly analysis of the Swedish labour movement's achievements became directly connected to Carmichael's quest for a new political vision. After his 1985 visit to Sweden representing the ACTU, Carmichael expressed his profound gratitude to his hosts, the Swedish Metal Workers' Union. He stated that the Australian labour movement was moving 'in the direction of policies and strategies that your organisation has already established and largely implemented. Of course they have to be applied in the concrete Australian circumstances. Nevertheless, we have very much to learn from you, which we must explore fully in as short a space of time as possible'.[42]

Carmichael reported that the Swedish unions' wages solidarity policy was 'the foundation stone of their policy development'. He commended their efforts for study leave, which 'raises productivity' and 'challenges and changes power relations on the job'. Moreover,

---

41 Winton Higgins, 'Political Unionism and the Corporatist Thesis', *Economic and Industrial Democracy*, Vol. 6, No. 3, 1985, pp. 355, 356–357, 354, 359, 360–361, 367, 369, 363.

42 Letter of 9 December 1985 in the records of the Swedish Metal Workers' Union, Stockholm.

they constantly stress the importance of the political dimension of their work and the use of legislative power to magnify their industrial organisation. They have highly developed... connections into...political processes starting from their remarkable community discussion groups apparatus up to fortnightly government-trade union consultations.

He warned that this

does not mean that the...unions...achieve all they set out to achieve at any given time. Sometimes the results are less...than they believe they should be...but it is clearly apparent that their position is always continuously developing with perspective about it.

Carmichael also reported on the co-determination legislation and its provisions for union representatives on company boards, supported by education programs, and on the legislative establishment of renewal funds, following negotiations between Swedish unions and management, into which companies with certain levels of profits were required to devote some resources to 'promot[e]...industrial democracy...education, skill, responsibility and cultural capacity' for their employees.

Further, he reported that the

industrial democracy movement starting along with other democratic explosions of development from the mid-[19] 60s [occurred] to challenge the denial of working people from having a say in decision-making and in particular, the most vicious form of this denial, in the work process itself.

Carmichael suggested that current industrial trends 'create...a big...opportunity to negotiate better working conditions and work practices' and that, in their attitude to this opportunity, the Swedish unions had placed themselves 'in the forefront of the world's working-class movements'. Volvo provided a 'dramatic example' for Carmichael, in particular the new plant underway at Uddevalla to replace the former shipyards, in which 'groups of up to thirty workers with…high…levels of skills, with thirty minute planned work cycles and not more than 50 per cent of anybody's time on routine assembly, will be involved'. To sum up, he stated that:

> I believe there is so much to learn from their experience. Particularly in relation to Labor being in government and what expectations the…unions should have…
>
> Of all the countries I have had the chance to visit, Sweden emerges as being the most valuable to learn from in relation to a Labor government being in office…it leads me to *express a view as strongly as I can that a small representative…delegation from the ACTU through LO should seek to visit Sweden* to undertake a more detailed study of the matters I have only had the opportunity to explore in general terms and to study matters about which I did not have the time to examine.[43]

Thus in this short visit in 1985 – and in the following year's longer visit as a leading member of the delegation for which he lobbied, which would produce the major 1987 report titled *Australia Reconstructed* – Carmichael became very enthusiastic about the political possibilities which Sweden showed. This influenced him into renewed support for and perseverance with the Accord, despite its shortcomings, in an attempt to achieve the kind of things which the Swedish unions had through their 'political unionism'.

Public disputes between Left unions and the government over its failure to implement important elements of the Accord continued in

---

43   Laurie Carmichael, National Research Officer, AMWU, 'Report to ACTU Officers', n.d. c. late 1985/early 1986: Noel Butlin Archives Centre, Deposit Z102, Box 555 ('Industrial Democracy 1985–1986'). Emphasis in the original.

Australia, and Carmichael continued to participate in them up to a point. However, in the end, he emphasised that 'it is…up to the labour movement to revive the Accord to save the Government…the union movement cannot simply be critical. There must be effective campaigning to change [the] course of the Government's self-destructive policies'.[44] The *Australia Reconstructed* mission became a central part of the campaigning effort which Carmichael and colleagues would make.

Olle Hammarström drew on his extensive networks among senior Swedish union leaders to put together a very substantial itinerary for the visiting 1986 Australian delegation.[45]

The influence of Sweden had become noticeable enough by August 1986 that a leading academic in the political economy movement, Frank Stilwell, began to raise concern about 'Carmichael's…view which builds on notions of 'political unionism' developed particularly in Sweden and discussed in the Australian context in various writings by Winton Higgins'. This view was that 'the Accord could have…the potential not only for generating absolute and relative gains in the material living standards of the working class but also for opening up hitherto unprecedented access to political power'. Stilwell reiterated earlier Left scepticism about social democratic 'collaboration', stating that, 'the "Swedish road to socialism" remained a hotly contested issue' and that the Carmichael 'perspective of the Accord is simply optimism…that, because an agreement such as the Accord opens up avenues for unions to be involved in the formulation of government policy, this can lead to benefits for the working class, broadly defined,

---

44   *The Metal Worker* (newspaper), Sydney, May 1986.
45   Hammarström interview.

in the short term and/or conditions more conducive to a socialist transition in the longer term'.[46]

The point however is that the picture which Carmichael had formed of Sweden gave him reasons for optimism. From August to September 1986, a high-level delegation from the ACTU went to Sweden, Norway, (what was then West) Germany, Austria and Britain to seek new policy options for Australia. The delegation's major report, *Australia Reconstructed*, was published in the following year. The report particularly praised and sought to emulate Sweden because of the overriding priority which that country placed on full employment and wage solidarity, while maintaining a strong economic performance.[47]

Days after his return from that visit to Stockholm, Carmichael was publicly spelling out his enthusiasm about the Swedish unions, the level of resources they enjoyed and their emphasis on education. His attendance of the Swedish LO congress had demonstrated to him 'the degree of commitment that the...union movement has to a sophisticated view of the economy'. He reported that:

> one third of the congress was given over to discussing problems of production. Now in our...union movement, the amount of discussion of production would be lucky if it was two or three per cent of the period of Congress. You would have a discussion about the economy, but it would be largely about what we would expect the Government to do about it and very little about what we expect the...union movement to do.[48]

---

46   Frank Stilwell, *The Accord – and Beyond*, Pluto Press Australia, Sydney, 1986, p. 28.
47   Australian Council of Trade Unions (ACTU) and Trade Development Council (TDC), *Australia Reconstructed: ACTU/TDC Mission to Western Europe: A Report by the Mission Members to the ACTU and the TDC*, Australian Government Publishing Service, Canberra, 1987.
48   'Carmichael's Swedish Message to Unions', *Financial Review*, Sydney, 6 October 1986.

Further, he related how in Sweden:

> labour market policy...is a major cornerstone of the...unions' work...unions are told of intended plant closures and their main effort is directed not at redundancy deals, but at retraining workers and restructuring industry...[As well,] there is expanded power of the shop stewards to intervene in production and investment.[49]

In the nine-month period until the publication of the full *Australia Reconstructed* report in July 1987, the delegation's researchers followed up their findings. Ted Wilshire and other members of a team of researchers worked intensively through that time in a suite of Department of Trade offices in central Sydney to write up the many features of Sweden which the unions had come to admire, as the main theme of the 235-page, A4-sized official-looking volume titled *Australia Reconstructed*. The report included more than 100 colour charts to illustrate statistical trends, policy concepts, and organisational arrangements; it made 72 substantial policy recommendations; and it had a bibliography with more than 300 references. As the publication was being edited, Wilshire enlisted Winton Higgins to help.[50] Wilshire also sent the manuscript to Bill Ford, who played a proofreading and editorial role in *Australia Reconstructed* though he did not have any primary policy input.[51]

Australia Reconstructed was printed prior to, but not released until after, Australia's 1987 national election, at which the Labor Government was re-elected for a third term.

---

49   'European Example is Path to Follow, says Carmichael', *The Metal Worker*, November 1986.
50   Higgins interview.
51   Ford interview.

The 1986 visit and the resulting 1987 *Australia Reconstructed* report represent the most prominent interest in the Nordic nations in Australian political history to date. *Australia Reconstructed* also remains the most comprehensive policy manifesto ever published by the mainstream Left in Australia. Its contents have been widely discussed.

The publication continued the concern about Australia's excessive economic reliance on extracting and shipping out resources rather than adding value to products, which had been expressed in a series of earlier pamphlets published from the second half of the 1970s by the AMWU. Following those publications, which had criticised Australia's policy direction in the Fraser Right-of-centre Government years (1975–1983), the union delegation put forward positive policy solutions in *Australia Reconstructed* for the Australian Labor Party Government to pursue.

Although the 1986 mission to Europe was partly sponsored by – and its report published with the official imprimatur of – the then Hawke Labor Government, it contained much criticism of that government's policies. The authors emphasised the achievements made by Sweden's Rehn-Meidner model in pursuing full employment by reducing market wage differentials, ensuring an adequate social wage, and improving the mobility and skills of the labour force through comprehensive, active labour-market measures. They argued that this approach had succeeded in Sweden from the 1950s because unions had rejected 'the notion that wage restraint was the only solution, and instead [had] urged the Social Democratic government to adopt an alternative strategy involving the whole policy mix'.[52]

---

52   Australian Council of Trade Unions and Trade Development Council, *Australia Reconstructed*, p. 5.

CHAPTER 1

The Australian trade union delegates did not visit Denmark or Finland, but they were impressed by the vast resources invested in vocational training to develop a highly skilled workforce in what was then West Germany. The unionists commented favourably on the way that improving the skill base of the workforce was not regarded in Germany as a last resort defensive activity, undertaken to relieve temporary skill shortages or to cope with the threat of retrenchments, but was an essential component of long-term business strategies for international competitive advantage.[53]

Australia Reconstructed represented the most ambitious attempt towards economic interventionism in the Hawke/Keating years (1983–1996). It sought to develop the original logic, new institutions, and progressive aspects of the Prices and Incomes Accord signed by the ALP and the ACTU in February 1983, which had envisaged a regulated economy and a high priority for industry development. In particular, *Australia Reconstructed* sought to counter the Government's moves to financial deregulation and away from industry policy in the years following the signing of the Accord, which were contrary to the Accord's original agreed provisions. Among the policy proposals in *Australia Reconstructed* was a call for restraint of prices and executive salaries instead of just wages. It advocated the development of manufacturing by using new superannuation funds to promote productive investment, among other measures. It called for better formation of vocational skills. It also endorsed the reorganisation of work along more democratic lines.

The year in which the report appeared, 1987, preceded the waves of privatisations, further tariff reductions, and shifts away from

53   Ibid., pp. xiii, 108, 118.

centralised wage fixing that came later in the Hawke/Keating years. As such, *Australia Reconstructed* remains an important reference point for an alternative and more interventionist Labor political and economic approach that came to dominate the period 1983–1996.

Australia Reconstructed was, of course, criticised at the time by employers. The Business Council of Australia sent its own mission to Sweden, the month after the union delegates returned, to paint a contrary picture. Leading 'Dries' suggested that the ACTU was engaging in Nordic hero worship; and one suggested that proposals to involve trade unions more broadly in national policy making would inevitably make Australia akin to Fascist Italy under Mussolini.[54] Apparently none of those who made this second charge appreciated the distinction between the capricious actions of an Italian dictator before the Second World War and *social democratic* corporatism as it had gradually and successfully evolved in northern European nations in the decades after the War.

Another repeated complaint about *Australia Reconstructed*, made by the leader of the largest employer organisation of the time, was that it was too hard to read.[55] This was somewhat odd coming from an organisation whose members had regularly called for higher literacy standards among young people.

Not all criticism came from the employer side, however. Community welfare activists criticised the report for not placing nearly enough emphasis on the role which public-sector provision had

54 John Hyde, 'ACTU Corporatism Was a Failure in Mussolini's Italy', *The Australian*, Sydney, 28 August 1987.

55 Pamela Williams, 'ACTU Report Branded as Dangerous by CAI Head', *Financial Review*, Sydney, 17 September 1987, quoting Bryan Noakes, then director general of the Confederation of Australian Industry; Confederation of Australian Industry 1987, *Employer Perspectives on the ACTU/TDC Report "Australia Reconstructed"*, Confederation of Australian Industry, Melbourne, 1987.

played in Sweden's success, and also for viewing the social wage too narrowly.[56] Further, the report's focus on manufacturing industry and skills training policy, while that reflected the priorities of the main participating unionists, limited the report's scope. Although *Australia Reconstructed* did outline in detail the laws and programs that Sweden introduced to combat labour-market segmentation and to promote equal wages and conditions for women, and did strongly recommend similar moves in Australia, it did not adequately analyse the services sector of employment where most women were actually employed. Nor did its recommendations reflect women's need for childcare.[57] The document was also criticised by conservationists for purporting to 'encompass the major debates of our time' while essentially ignoring environmental questions.[58]

It has been argued that *Australia Reconstructed* did not succeed because it was an 'attempt to transpose northern European social democratic programs into a society [here] which lacks the cultural and institutional background to embrace those programs'.[59]

Trade unions in Sweden had participated at a high level in national policy-making in Sweden since the landmark Saltsjöbaden Agreement of 1938 (so named because it was reached in the seaside resort town of Saltsjöbaden, south-east of Stockholm). This did entrench processes there to an extent very difficult for an Australian government coming

56   Council of Social Service of New South Wales, '*Australia Reconstructed*: What's in It for the Community Services Industry?', Council of Social Service of New South Wales, Sydney, 1988.

57   Pat Ranald, 'Unions Unreconstructed?', *Australian Left Review*, No.105, 1988, pp. 10–11.

58   Phillip Toyne, 'Trade Unions and the Environment' in *Labour Movement Strategies for the 21st Century*, Evatt Foundation, Sydney, 1991, p. 27.

59   Editorial, 'Australia Reconstructed: 10 Years On', *Journal of Australian Political Economy*, No. 39, 1997, p. 2.

into office in the early 1980s to match, even if it had been genuinely committed to a wide-ranging partnership with trade unions. However, central figures in the Hawke and Keating Governments, and some senior officials in the ACTU hierarchy closest to them, never did genuinely consider or pursue the recommendations in *Australia Reconstructed*.[60] The big difference between the Accord as practised in Australia from 1983, and Swedish social corporatism over the preceding decades, is that the political side of the labour movement in Sweden acted far more in the spirit of the agreements with the trade unions than did their counterparts in Australia in the 1980s and 1990s.

Australian Labor governments chose instead to follow the intellectually fashionable market liberal policies urged on them by powerful business constituencies and by the advocates of those policies in the commercial media and in the senior public service.

Nevertheless, *Australia Reconstructed* was generally acknowledged as a sophisticated and somewhat surprising challenge to conventional economic policy thinking in Australia. Debate over the report was prominent in the national media from the time of its launch in July 1987. A series of visiting government ministers and other officials from Sweden and Norway helped to keep Nordic nations' alternative economic and industrial policy approach before the Australian public for some months.

On 19 October 1987 the stock market crash shifted attention away from *Australia Reconstructed* – although the collapse of the overvalued speculative activity was one of the very things the union delegation had been foreshadowing. The report had expressed concern at 'the

---

60   Evan Jones, 'Background to *Australia Reconstructed*' ibid. pp. 17–38.

impact...the recent wave of takeovers...is having on the level and composition of investment undertaken by the real production and value-adding sectors of the economy'. It recommended that the Australian Government follow the lead of the governments in the Nordic nations, which were acting to remedy this problem by 'supplementing private sector activities through collective capital formation...[for] investment in...infrastructure, education...training and capital works'.[61]

In 1986, the same year that Carmichael and the other Australian trade unionists were in Stockholm, Canadian political scientist Henry Milner was also there, researching for a book which would be titled *Sweden: Social Democracy in Practice*. Many of Milner's findings were similar to those made by the Australian trade union delegates. He was impressed by what he called Sweden's 'solidaristic market economy'. He argued that Swedes had achieved comparative social equality with economic prosperity because of their distinctive sense of a

> complementary rather than contradictory relationship of the[se] two spheres. For Swedes...the very possibility of maintaining a community where...human relations are based on social solidarity...is understood as conditional upon the community's 'fitness' at surviving in the international economic jungle...The institutionalised social solidarity around them enables Swedes to feel secure and thus prepared to follow the market in the promising directions it opens up.[62]

Similarly, *Australia Reconstructed* had observed that

---

61 Australian Council of Trade Unions and Trade Development Council, *Australia Reconstructed*, pp. 14, 19–20.
62 Milner, *Sweden: Social Democracy in Practice*, Oxford University Press, Oxford, 1989, pp. 16–17.

people threatened by adjustments which may force them to accept unemployment, job transfers or lower wages, will obviously oppose change. People with financial security are far better able to see changes as positive opportunities. The Swedes...see a need to protect workers forced out of declining industries. In consequence, they have developed...generous unemployment insurance, social welfare, early warning of retrenchments and incentives to retrain, enhance skills and relocate. Rapid structural change can then become an avenue to increased career opportunities rather than a threat.[63]

Milner acknowledged that Sweden's 'small size and relative cultural homogeneity' were factors conducive to solidarity. But he also emphasised the role that 'the actions and teachings of the SAP' had played in shaping 'the wide range of publicly oriented...activities... of Swedish voluntary associations...[into] a 'buffer zone' between the marketplace on the one side and the state bureaucracy on the other'. In Sweden, said Milner, this 'buffer zone is especially wide due to the participation by representatives of unions, business, and other interest organisations on publicly-mandated boards, agencies, and commissions, and the provision of important services to the public by the interest organisations themselves'. 'The knowledge required to live full, rich lives as members of their community and as human beings...is woven into the very fabric of Swedish institutions,' he wrote. 'An informed, educated populace...means a significant reduction in uncertainty. Sweden achieves this notably through free public education at all levels, a major effort at adult education, publicly owned communications media, and heavy expenditures on libraries, museums and popular culture'. Milner also emphasised Sweden's

---

63   Australian Council of Trade Unions and Trade Development Council, *Australia Reconstructed*, p. 105.

CHAPTER 1

encouragement of research and development.[64] Similarly, *Australia Reconstructed* drew attention to the fact that in Sweden the Volvo motor company alone invested as much in research and development as did Australia's entire private sector.[65]

Henry Milner has continued to positively present the Nordic nations' policy achievements since his 1986 visit, while acknowledging that some setbacks have occurred. He has updated and widened his analysis with further books and became a regular visiting professor at Sweden's Umeå University. He has emphasised the continuing strength and political importance of what he characterises as the advanced degree of 'civic literacy' in Nordic nations. A well-informed citizenry is of crucial importance in sustaining the Nordic nations' welfare states, Milner argues.[66]

A book by an American political scientist, which positively analysed the enduring nature of the Swedish social democrats' *ideological* achievement, appeared one year after Milner's first book about Sweden.[67]

There was a major public debate about the *Australia Reconstructed* publication from July to October 1987. Laurie Carmichael led the case for its policy recommendations. He had regularly to rebut accusations that it was seeking the 'Swedenisation' of Australia. Carmichael held the position of ACTU Assistant Secretary until September 1991. During and after this, he continued his campaign for the skills training components of the *Australia Reconstructed* manifesto. The

64 Milner, *Sweden: Social Democracy in Practice*, 1989, pp. 19, 74, 154, 42.
65 Australian Council of Trade Unions and Trade Development Council, *Australia Reconstructed*, p. 87.
66 Henry Milner, *Civic Literacy: How Informed Citizens Make Democracy Work*, University Press of New England, Hanover, New Hampshire, 2002.
67 Tim Tilton, *The Political Theory of Swedish Social Democracy: Through the Welfare State to Socialism*, Oxford University Press, Oxford, 1990.

favourable impression of Sweden he had formed in 1985 and 1986 sustained him throughout these efforts.

Swedish arrangements in some modest ways came to influence Australia's agenda for training reform, known as 'Award Restructuring'. Several further, smaller-scale visits by Australian unionists and researchers in the later 1980s contributed to detailed debate on issues including skills reclassification – but their policy ambition was nowhere near as great as *Australia Reconstructed*. They were like sequels to a blockbuster. Also, a group of AMWU researchers who had been supportive of the initial Accord (because of its potential for social democratic policy interventions), of the political achievements of Nordic unions and of goals for humanising the workplace through enhanced training opportunities, in the early 1990s broke away from, and criticised, the ACTU and the Labor Government. Their criticism was that key union leaders and the government were no longer pursuing those goals, the stated industry policy objectives, nor the recommendations made by *Australia Reconstructed*, because they had been overwhelmed by a contrary, employer-driven agenda for enterprise level bargaining.[68] That agenda would, in turn, usher in an era of work intensification and worse inequalities to Australia.

Winton Higgins shared these critics' concerns.[69] He considers that the 'Swedish model' 'lost a lot in translation' to Australia in the later 1980s, although for this he does not criticise Laurie Carmichael. Rather, he sees Carmichael as trying to achieve what was possible in

---

68   Peter Ewer, Ian Hampson, Chris Lloyd, John Rainford, Steve Rix and Meg Smith, *Politics and the Accord*, Pluto Press Australia, Sydney, 1991, pp. 111–117 and passim.

69   See for example Winton Higgins, 'Missing the Boat: Labor and Industry in the Eighties' in Brian Galligan and Gwynneth Singleton (eds.), *Business and Government Under Labor*, Longman Cheshire, Melbourne, 1991, pp. 102–117.

a political context which rapidly became very adverse and dominated by neo-liberal economics.[70]

Australia was not reconstructed in accordance with the image of Sweden formed by the Australian unionists who went there in the mid-1980s. Nevertheless, the Australian trade unionists' interest during the 1980s in the policy approaches taken by Sweden, Norway and other northern European nations was commendably outward-looking and visionary. The *Australia Reconstructed* publication continued the interest in Sweden shown by the Left in other countries including by British Fabians in various decades, by US academic John D. Stephens in the late 1970s (to whose writings the publication includes explicit references) and by Canadian political scientist Henry Milner in the 1980s.

Many critics from the Right of politics in English-speaking countries gleefully pronounced the 'Swedish model' dead in the 1990s, arguing (for example, in regular articles in the market liberal magazine *The Economist*) that the sharp rise in unemployment in Sweden then was an inevitable result of excessive regulation and welfare provision. The assassination of Sweden's brilliant Social Democratic Prime Minister, Olof Palme, in 1986, the SAP's election defeat in 1991, and the international recession of the 1990s – which included the Nordic nations – led many to proclaim the end of the 'Swedish model'.

However, the SAP quickly returned to office, in 1994, and governed until 2006. Although that SAP government under Göran Persson did adopt some neo-liberal policies, other analysts have argued – convincingly – that 'the model' has survived, that it has adapted and prospered and that Sweden continues to offer a substantial

70   Higgins interview.

and successful alternative to the predominant policy approaches in English-speaking nations.[71]

An American-born and long-time Australian-based social policy academic, Professor Sheila Shaver, expressed confidence in the Nordic nations' distinctive achievements, drawing on her first-hand study of Sweden in 1997–1998 (as the Kerstin Hesselgren Visiting Professor at Umeå and Stockholm universities). Shaver pointed out the continuing 'high levels of public employment especially of women' and 'the more robust conceptions [of equality] institutionalised in Scandinavian welfare states'. She contended that 'Nordic welfare reform had kept faith with its tradition of universalistic egalitarianism' in contrast to the more conditional and residual character of welfare reform in Australia, particularly following the election of the Howard Right-of-centre Government.[72]

The persistent merits of social democratic Sweden were also recognised by the energetic Compass grouping in the British Labour Party in 2005, following the disappointment with the Blair 'New Labour' government's failure to significantly reduce inequality.[73]

More surprisingly, in 2006 the Business Council of Australia came to praise the continuing Nordic commitment to skills formation, support of high-tech manufacturing industry, and investment in research and development, in a policy statement on innovation.[74] This was in

71   Peter H. Lindert, *Growing Public: Social Spending and Economic Growth since the Eighteenth Century*, Cambridge University Press, New York, 2004, Vol. 1, Ch. 11.

72   Sheila Shaver, 'Welfare, Equality and Globalisation: Reconceiving Social Citizenship' in Keith Horton and Haig Patapan (eds.), *Globalisation and Equality*, Routledge, London, 2004, pp. 99, 102, 111, 100.

73   Robert Taylor, *Sweden's New Social Democratic Model: Proof That a Better World is Possible*, Compass, London, 2005.

74   Business Council of Australia, *New Pathways to Prosperity: A National Innovation Framework for Australia*, Business Council of Australia, Melbourne, 2006, pp. 12, 17, 18, 19, 20.

marked contrast to its critical response to the major Australian trade union report on Nordic policy achievements two decades earlier. Thus the main critic of the Australian unions' portrayal of the Nordic nations following their 1986 visit itself eventually repeated some aspects of this positive portrayal. This suggests that the substance of the Nordic nations' achievements presented in *Australia Reconstructed* was more accurate, and of more long-term relevance to Australia, than the initial reaction against it implied.

Similarly, in 2013, *The Economist* magazine was obliged by the weight of evidence to issue a much more positive assessment of the Nordic nations' achievements than it had done two decades previously. This included acknowledgement of the Nordic nations' above average economic growth from the 1990s and the fact that they had, essentially, maintained their traditional generous welfare states in addition to their successes in technological innovation.[75]

The Australian academics Winton Higgins and Geoff Dow have gone on to recently complete a comprehensive study of Ernst Wigforss, the intellectual turned politician who was Sweden's treasurer from 1932 to 1949 in the Social Democratic Party governments, his remarkable legacy and the continuing inspiration which his contribution provides.[76]

There remains a careful but consistent argument for the continuing important differences between national industrial relations approaches even in the age of 'globalisation' and a still hopeful outlook on the possibilities for and benefits of industrial democracy; with the

75 'Northern Lights: Special Report: The Nordic Countries', *The Economist* (magazine), London, 2 February 2013.
76 Geoff Dow and Winton Higgins, *Politics against Pessimism: Social Democratic Possibilities since Ernst Wigforss*, PIE-Peter Lang, Bern, 2013.

Nordic nations in each case still being seen as leading exemplars.[77] Nordic nations are again now attracting interest for their distinctive achievements in a range of policy areas. Emissaries from – as well as to – the Nordic nations are influencing policy debates in English-speaking countries.

Australians are again among those seeking to learn from, and to advocate the lessons from, Nordic nations' achievements which may be learned by the English-speaking world. Chapters 2 to 5 outline some of those contemporary policy achievements and lessons in detail.

77 Åke Sandberg (ed.), *Nordic Lights: Work, Management and Welfare in Scandinavia*, SNS Förlag, Stockholm, 2013.

Chapter 2

SWEDEN'S LEADING ROLE IN REDUCING CHILD POVERTY AND IMPROVING CHILDREN'S WELLBEING

The proportion of children living in income poverty in Australia is nearly 11 per cent, whereas in the four main Nordic nations – Sweden, Finland, Denmark and Norway – this figure averages just over 6 per cent, according to the United Nations Children's Fund (UNICEF). The Nordic nations clearly lead the world in having the lowest proportion of children who suffer from deprivation.[1] Sweden and the other main Nordic nations provide an example of how societies can make policy choices to lift many more children out of poverty than Australia presently does. This chapter aims to identify what Australia can learn from this example to reduce poverty and inequality, and increase wellbeing, among children.

Sweden has long been known for the priority which it gives to meeting children's needs and enshrining children's rights. Its leading role in this respect has been attributed, in an important 1990s essay

---

1   UNICEF, *Measuring Child Poverty: New League Tables of Child Poverty in the World's Rich Countries*, UNICEF Innocenti Research Centre, Florence, 2012, pp. 3, 2.

by Göran Therborn, as resulting in part from the strong early presence in Sweden and its neighbouring countries of egalitarian individualist values. Also important is the fact that the Lutheran religion to which most citizens of Nordic nations are nominally affiliated has been less influential than the Catholic and Orthodox religions have been in other countries, which meant that patriarchal norms were weakened in Sweden compared to other countries. In addition, there is the fact that Sweden's civil law (as distinct from other countries' common law) tradition ensured that egalitarian individualist principles were expressed relatively rapidly and fully in formal national rules. 'The Nordic configuration of religion, law, and patriarchy provided a favourable cultural context for the modern world's first advance towards children's rights in the 1910s–1920s,' Therborn wrote. These advances 'met less resistance than elsewhere' and, in Sweden, as in the other Nordic countries, the 'legal system…was uniquely open to novel, egalitarian and individualist conceptions'. Its 'politico-legal-decision-making…was very favourable to legal change' for children's rights.[2]

Similar points were emphasised when a leading Swedish paediatrician was asked recently to summarise for an Australian audience the reasons for his country's policy achievements for children. Professor Staffan Janson, from Sweden's Karlstad University, drew attention to the cultural comparisons made of where different countries stand, from survival values to self-expression values, and from traditional or more religious values to more secular-rational values. These comparisons show that self-expression and secular-rational values are

---

2   Göran Therborn, 'The Politics of Childhood: The Rights of Children in Modern Times' in Francis G. Castles (ed.), *Families of Nations: Patterns of Public Policy in Western Democracies*, Dartmouth, Aldershot, 1993, pp. 266, 270–272, 273, 274, 277, 278.

highest in Sweden and the other Nordic nations. There is widespread awareness of the positive benefits of socio-economic equality in Sweden, and there is greater gender equality between women and men in Sweden than in nearly all other countries. In the context of a positive view of the active role which the government should play in many aspects of life, there is also a strong sense of individual rights in Sweden. Children have long been seen as individuals in their own right.[3]

Sweden's achievements for children include its having one of the smallest proportions in the world of low birth-weight children i.e. of newborn babies weighing less than 2,500 grams (or 2.5 kilograms or 5.5 pounds). Low birth weights are a negative indicator for infant health. In Sweden, the proportion of newborn children who have low birth weights is 4.2 per cent, whereas in Australia it is 6.2 per cent.[4]

In explaining Sweden's achievements for children, Janson emphasises preventative health care, support for highly skilled midwives and the compiling and consulting of comprehensive and accurate data about births. He further emphasises ensuring that all expectant mothers are seen early in their pregnancy and that action is taken to contact those who have not been seen by ten weeks into their pregnancy to help them cope with any social problems which may have caused that delay. Parenting classes to prepare for delivery have been provided in Sweden since the early 1970s for fathers as well as for mothers. The Social Democratic Party governments' program, to build a million new dwellings from 1965 to 1974 so that reasonably priced

3   Staffan Janson, 'An Overview of Nordic Policy for Children: Lessons for Australia on How to Reduce Inequalities' in Andrew Scott (ed.), *Changing Children's Chances: Can Australia Learn from Nordic Countries?*, Centre for Citizenship and Globalisation, Deakin University, Melbourne, 2012, pp. 12–21.
4   OECD, *Health at a Glance 2013*, OECD, Paris, 2013, pp. 39, 38.

modern housing would be available to nearly everybody, played an important part in boosting the living conditions in which Swedish children have grown up. Also important was the near-universal expansion of – and parents' participation in – 'Well-Baby Clinics' which closely monitor the health and progress of newborn babies.

Further, as part of general concern for ensuring mothers' and babies' good nutrition, there has been detailed work in Sweden to support breastfeeding. The World Health Organisation regards exclusive breastfeeding for the first six months to be best for babies everywhere. Sweden's breastfeeding rates have risen to near the highest in the world with a ranking on the Breastfeeding Policy Scorecard of 9.6 out of 10 or Very Good, compared with New Zealand's 7.6 and Britain's 7.2, which are Good; Canada's 5.4, which is Fair; and Australia's 4.8 and the United States' 4.2, which are Poor.[5]

The prospects of children surviving birth and the first year of life are much higher in Sweden than nearly all other countries. Whereas the probability that a child born will die before reaching the age of one (the 'infant mortality rate') is only 2.1 for every 1,000 births in Sweden, in Australia it is 3.8; in Britain it is 4.1; in Canada it is 4.9; in New Zealand it is 5.5; while it is 6.1 in the United States.[6]

Infant mortality is lower in Sweden and the other Nordic nations than elsewhere in the world in part because those nations have a 'dual earner' (or dual breadwinner) support policy. This is based on a norm of both men and women undertaking paid work. It combines welfare universalism with an employment orientation. Dual earner support is designed to allow mothers and fathers alike to participate

---

5   Save the Children, *Nutrition in the First 1000 Days: State of the World's Mothers*, Save the Children USA, Westport, Connecticut, 2012, pp. 39, 43.

6   OECD, *Health at a Glance 2013*, p. 37.

in paid employment, through the provision of a long period of paid parental leave and public childcare services. The nations which pursue this policy differ from a second category of countries which pursue a 'general family' support policy, which involves giving money to the husband who tends to be working while the mother tends to stay at home. The 'general family' support policy relies on a highly gendered division of labour with subsidies to wage earners who have a dependent spouse. Neither the traditional 'general family' support policy nor the 'market oriented' family policy of the third category of countries, which includes Australia, reduces infant mortality to the low levels of the Nordic nations.[7] Australia has a one and a half breadwinner model which assumes a family structure of a male full-time worker and a female part-time worker. The proportion of employed women who work only part-time, instead of full-time, in Australia is double that of Sweden: 38.4 per cent compared with 18.6 per cent.[8] Women in Australia pay a price for tending to be so heavily in part-time work, rather than full-time work, in the form of downgraded career options and less pay and other benefits. The prospects of working women and of children will be improved if Australia becomes one of the 'dual earner' policy nations – with more women working in full-time jobs which have reasonable, regulated hours, or in more secure, better paid and higher quality part-time jobs which have better career prospects – like Sweden.

The 'child mortality rate', which means the probability that a newborn baby will die before reaching the age of five, is also low in

---

7   Olle Lundberg, Monica Åberg Yngwe, Maria Kölegård Stjärne, Jon Ivar Elstad, Tommy Ferrarini, Olli Kangas, Thor Norström, Joakim Palme and Johan Fritzell, 'The Role of Welfare State Principles and Generosity in Social Policy Programs for Public Health: An International Comparative Study', *The Lancet*, Vol. 372, No. 9650, November 2008, pp. 1633–1640.

8   *OECD Employment Outlook 2013*, Statistical Annex, Table H.

Sweden compared with other countries: three for every 1,000 births compared with five for every 1,000 births in Australia, Britain and Canada, six for every 1,000 births in New Zealand and seven for every 1,000 births in the US.[9]

'Australia's high child mortality is not explained by indigenous deaths because, although indigenous child mortality is approximately twice the non-indigenous rate, only 5.8 per cent of births are indigenous', Frank Shann, professor of critical care at the Royal Children's Hospital, Melbourne, points out.[10]

The mortality rates of indigenous – Aboriginal and Torres Strait Islander – children in Australia were double the rates of non-indigenous children in 2008, when a general policy of 'Closing the Gap' was adopted. This policy included a specific goal to halve the gap between the child mortality rates of indigenous and non-indigenous Australians by 2018. Current trends indicate that this specific goal may be met, although progress in closing the huge gaps between the life expectancy and employment outcomes of indigenous, and non-indigenous, Australians is not being made.[11] Australia's indigenous population numbers approximately 670,000. The Nordic nations also have an indigenous population: the approximately 100,000 Sami people who live across the northern parts of Sweden, Finland and Norway.[12] There is, by contrast with Australia, little sign of significant health problems among indigenous

9   UNICEF, *Levels and Trends in Child Mortality Report 2013: Estimates Developed by the UN Inter-agency Group for Child Mortality Estimation*, UNICEF, New York, 2013, pp. 16, 20, 22, 24.

10 *The Age*, Melbourne, 25 October 2013.

11 Australian Government, *Closing the Gap: Prime Minister's Report*, Commonwealth of Australia, Canberra, 2014, pp. 6, 8.

12 A small number of the Sami people also live across the Finnish border in what is now Russia.

children compared with non-indigenous children in the Nordic nations.[13]

Shann argues that 'Australia's high child mortality rate is probably due to *social,* rather than medical factors', and that we 'urgently need' to study Sweden, among other countries, 'to learn how to improve child survival in Australia'.[14]

Janson points to a very strong correlation between child mortality and income inequality in rich nations. An income inequality ratio comprising how much of a country's economic resources are used by the richest 20 per cent compared to the poorest 40 per cent shows that the higher the income inequality ratio in a given country, the higher is the under five mortality. The correlation is very high: 0.76 on a scale from 0 to 1 where 0 equals no correlation and 1 equals total correlation. Thus in less equal rich nations like Australia, children die before reaching the age of five at significantly higher rates than in more equal rich nations like Sweden.[15]

In *The Spirit Level* book, epidemiology professors Richard Wilkinson and Kate Pickett demonstrate the importance of reducing inequality in order to enhance children's wellbeing. Eminent paediatricians – notably Professor Jack Shonkoff with his neuroscience research on the developing brain – have previously provided clear evidence that investment is vitally needed in the early years of life. Economists – notably Professor James Heckman – have also shown that such investment delivers particularly strong returns for the community

---

13 Per Sjölander, 'What Is Known about the Health and Living Conditions of the Indigenous People of Northern Scandinavia, the Sami?', *Global Health Action*, Vol. 4, 2011, pp. 1–11.

14 *The Age*, Melbourne, 25 October 2013 (my emphasis).

15 David Collison, Colin Dey, Gwen Hannah and Lorna Stevenson, 'Income Inequality and Child Mortality in Wealthy Nations', *Journal of Public Health*, Vol. 29, No. 2, 2007, pp. 114–117.

through successful health, educational and other outcomes and reduced need for costly interventions in later life. Shonkoff's and Heckman's findings have been incorporated into a number of important reports since the OECD's first *Starting Strong* volume was issued in 2001.[16] Along with the work of Wilkinson and Pickett, those findings have great implications for the economic and social policies which governments should now pursue.

Sweden takes an approach of public health prevention of the societal, family and parenting risk factors for maltreatment of children. The US on the other hand places little emphasis on prevention and much on reaction: i.e. it has high levels of child-protection activity, removing at-risk children from their families and placing them in out-of-home care after individual instances of child maltreatment have occurred. Britain, Australia, Canada and New Zealand are in-between. The question is: do the English-speaking countries just want to continue to increase activity by child protection services, or do they want to do more to *prevent* occurrence in the first place? Preventative interventions on a societal and neighbourhood level can be more effective, including cost effective, for improving children's wellbeing.[17]

Sweden also now has the lowest childhood injury rates in the world. It has achieved this in part through widespread education programs for safety at home, and by making children's safety an integral part of community planning, to ensure among other things that children are

---

16   OECD, *Doing Better for Children*, OECD, Paris, 2009, pp. 66–69, 169, 179–180; OECD, *Starting Strong II: Early Childhood Education and Care*, OECD, Paris, 2006, pp. 88, 89, 232, 255–256; OECD, *Starting Strong III: A Quality Toolbox for Early Childhood Education and Care*, OECD, Paris, 2012, p. 34.

17   Ruth Gilbert, 'A Public Health Approach to Child Maltreatment: Sweden Still Leads the Way' in Martin McKee (ed.), *For the Sake of the Children: Social Paediatrics in Action*, Karlstad University Press, Karlstad, 2012, pp. 154–164.

CHAPTER 2

protected from the risks of car traffic.[18] Another reason for Sweden's low injury rate is that it has been illegal for more than three decades for anyone to hit a child in Sweden. Janson credits Sweden's early valuing of children as individuals in their own right for helping to prepare the ground for Sweden's world-leading decision in 1979 to ban all physical violence against children.

Reliable and up-to-date data comparing child homicide rates between countries is difficult to assemble, but the results of a 2009 study published in the *Medical Journal of Australia* show that, between 1987 and 2001, 437 Australian children aged under 15 years were victims of homicide, whereas in Sweden 103 were. Thus, Sweden, though it had, on average, nearly one half the size of the population of Australia over that period, had less than a quarter of the number of child homicides. More than one-third of the child homicides in Australia were identified as fatal child abuse, usually at home. The compilers of this data contend that 'lives could be saved by measures that reduce the incidence of child abuse' such as prohibiting all physical violence against children.[19] Banning physical violence against children would reduce the likelihood of parental 'discipline' getting out of control and of children being injured or killed. It would also reduce the risks of other lasting emotional or psychological damage being done to children who, instead of feeling securely attached to a parent, grow to fear that parent and to associate that parent with pain. Sweden emphasises the importance of

18 Vibeke Jansson, 'Why Does Sweden have the Lowest Childhood Injury Mortality in the World? The Roles of Architecture and Public Preschool Services', *Journal of Public Health Policy*, Vol. 27, No. 2, 2006, pp. 146–165.

19 Olav B. Nielssen, Matthew M. Large, Bruce D. Westmore and Steven M. Lackersteen, 'Child Homicide in New South Wales from 1991 to 2005', *Medical Journal of Australia*, Vol. 190, No. 1, 2009, pp. 7–10.

providing security in childhood, because if children feel secure then they are more likely to enjoy a full, rich, imaginative childhood. The only English-speaking country to ban all physical violence against children is New Zealand, which did so in 2007, partly in response to a high rate of child homicides. Australia and all English-speaking countries – apart from New Zealand – are thus still lagging behind other countries in protecting children from physical violence at the hands of parents.

The ban in Sweden since 1979 of any physical violence against children is well known and is seen by many as an inspiring policy. So was Sweden being the first developed nation to ratify the 1989 United Nations Convention on the Rights of the Child. In 1993, Sweden created an ombudsman for children. Norway had been the first country to do so. The word 'ombudsman' is itself a Swedish word from an Old Norse word essentially meaning 'representative'. The spread of general ombudsman positions around the world, since their inception in Sweden in the early 19th century to enable individuals to have their interests represented to, and protected against adverse actions by, public authorities, is one example of a positive policy in a Nordic nation which has already been followed elsewhere.[20] The decision by 34 countries, so far, to follow Sweden's 1979 ban on any physical violence against children is another such example.[21] The spread of children's ombudsman or children's commissioner positions from their inception in Scandinavia – including to some jurisdictions in Australia so far – is another.

20   Roy Gregory and Philip Giddings (eds.), *Righting Wrongs: The Ombudsman in Six Continents*, International Institute of Administrative Sciences, Amsterdam, 2000.
21   Joan E. Durrant and Anne B. Smith (eds.), *Global Pathways to Abolishing Physical Punishment: Realising Children's Rights*, Routledge, New York, 2011, p. 4 and updates at http://www.endcorporalpunishment.org.

Provision of extensive paid parental leave in Sweden has long been a crucial part of enabling families to make genuine choices about how to manage their working lives and to balance these with time for family. In 1974 Sweden became the first country in the world to provide paid parental leave. This provision was explicitly broader than maternity leave, because the six months' paid leave for each family with a new child could be taken by either the mother or the father. In 1978 the duration was extended to nine months and in 1980 to 12 months. Since 1995 there have been 480 days' (16 months) paid leave available for each child, and since 2002 a minimum of 60 days must be used by each parent – the so-called designated father's two months – if the family is to gain the full leave entitlement. The parent on leave is paid 80 per cent of her/his salary for one year and then the amount reduces. In addition, each parent is entitled to take unpaid leave until a child is 18 months. Fathers in Sweden have been increasingly using this time. Forty per cent of fathers took leave in 2012, using approximately 24 per cent of the total parental leave. Mothers tend to take leave from the beginning and fathers slightly later, when breastfeeding reduces. Swedish parents are not required to use all their leave entitlements immediately. They can use some, then save the rest until later; however, they are required to use the leave prior to the child turning eight years of age.[22]

Australia, in 2011, finally left the United States behind as the only OECD country without any statutory, nationwide provision for paid maternity leave. The national government's decision to introduce a

---

22   Janson, 'An Overview of Nordic Policy for Children: Lessons for Australia on How to Reduce Inequalities', p. 16; Swedish Institute, *Facts about Sweden: Gender Equality*, Swedish Institute, Stockholm, 2013, p. 2.

form of national parental leave was a positive step. However, it was initially only for maternity leave; it was only for 18 weeks; and it only paid mothers at the minimum wage. It also did not require any real contribution from the many businesses which will benefit from the new arrangements in terms of regaining, rather than losing, skilled, experienced and valuable employees who are likely to return to work well motivated because they have been given consideration in their family lives.

A very modest 'Dad and Partner Pay' was added to Australia's initial maternity leave scheme to enable a paid paternity leave component to take effect in 2013. This provides for fathers and same-sex partners to take two weeks' paid leave after their child is born, also at the minimum wage. Despite mothers' increased workforce participation in Australia, there are still very gendered patterns of employment while looking after young children. While three-quarters of working mothers with a child under the age of eleven seek to arrange their work so they can also care for their children, less than half of fathers do so.[23]

Many fathers juggling work-life pressures in Australia are struggling to nurture bonds with their children. Even though many men do want to be more involved in raising and caring for their children, and children also want more time with their parents, pressures from work are pulling fathers and children away from one another. Half of fathers with young children in Australia work long hours, and nearly 60 per cent of fathers are feeling rushed or pressed for time. This, and the obstacles to their being able to reduce their working

---

23   See detailed data in Jennifer Baxter, *Parents Working Out Work*, Australian Institute of Family Studies, Melbourne, 2013, p. 9.

hours to the levels they want, is impeding Australian fathers' greater participation in parenting.[24]

Fathers who do take paternity leave, especially those who take two weeks or more, after the birth of a child are much more likely to be involved in the lives of their children, including regularly engaging in tasks such as feeding the child, changing nappies, getting up during the night to attend to the child, giving the child a bath, and reading bedtime stories to the child. There is also some evidence that children with highly involved fathers tend to perform better in terms of cognitive test scores.[25]

More extensive paternity leave will be needed in Australia to improve the combining of paid work with caring for children, to promote parental gender equality and to strengthen father/child relationships. Australia's parental leave arrangements, even after the small paternity leave component was added, remain minimal and need to be expanded in order to increase women's workforce participation.

The debate on the provision of more comprehensive paid parental leave in Australia has been distorted by the particular circumstances of party political positioning and electioneering, which led to the change of governing party in 2013. The leader of the Right-of-centre party, now Australia's prime minister, Tony Abbott, adopted when in opposition a policy for a more expansive, more universalist paid parental leave policy. This was at odds with his own previous,

---

24 Pocock, Skinner and Williams, *Time Bomb*, pp. 34–36; Natalie Skinner, Claire Hutchinson and Barbara Pocock, *The Big Squeeze: Work, Home and Care in 2012*, Centre for Work and Life, University of South Australia, Adelaide, 2012, pp. 12, 26–27, 36, 41, 45.

25 Maria del Carmen Huerta *et al, Fathers' Leave, Fathers' Involvement and Child Development: Are They Related? Evidence from Four OECD Countries*, OECD Social, Employment and Migration Working Papers, No. 140, OECD, Paris, 2013, pp. 39–41.

clearly stated personal views against paid parental leave, contrary to his general socially conservative philosophy and at odds also with the market liberal economic policy of his own party. Many see the switch as motivated by a desire to overcome his poor polling among women due to perceptions of him as a misogynist or as a person clinging to patriarchal norms. If the policy proceeds when planned in mid-2015, it will pay working women at their full salary up to a maximum salary level of $100,000, for six months' leave after the birth of a baby, funded in part by a bigger contribution from business (a 1.5 per cent levy on large corporations). Also, fathers will then be eligible to take their two weeks' leave at full salary (rather than at the minimum wage as at present). (The policy taken to the 2013 national election was for the maximum salary level of eligible working women to be $150,000, but this was reduced to $100,000 in the lead-up to Abbott Government's first budget in May 2014 due to urgent financial pressures claimed by Mr Abbott. The real reason for the reduction, however, may have been the ongoing campaign by market liberals inside the Liberal Party against Mr Abbott's paid parental leave policy.)

Some in-principle supporters of expanded paid parental leave have opposed this particular expansion in the context of a generally targeted welfare system, in which there are other priorities, including childcare, which may be weakened by spending so much on the more expansive paid parental leave scheme. Others have supported it. One reason for their support is that it will help upgrade the career options and help overcome the lesser pay and other benefits which women suffer over their working lives compared to men. Another is that it will increase breastfeeding in Australia towards the six months' duration which the World Health Organisation considers to be optimal. Australia's Work and Family Policy Roundtable Election Evaluation in August 2013 concluded in favour of the plan, despite misgivings about the details and credibility of its costings and about its singular focus on just one element in the suite of work/family policies which are needed. This situation creates a conundrum, which will be further discussed later in this chapter.

There is a very long interval between the end of the current eighteen weeks' paid maternity leave at the minimum wage for eligible families, plus the two weeks 'Dad and Partner' pay, and the start of preschool in Australia, which is usually at four years of age. There still will be a long interval from 2015, if and when the longer six months' paid parental leave scheme is introduced, between that six months and the time when a child starts preschool in Australia at age four.

In Sweden, since the mid-1990s, preschools and childcare services, though they developed separately, have increasingly been brought together as Early Childhood Education and Care (ECEC) services in recognition of the valuable social learning which takes place in settings formally designated as being for child-minding. All children in Sweden have a tax-funded ECEC place paid from central government funds and operated at the municipal level. There is a guarantee of three hours free ECEC services per day for all children from the time they turn one year old. Children are then entitled to 15 hours free ECEC services per week from the autumn term of the year in which they turn three years old until they start school. In Australia, despite the fact that the majority of mothers are back at work before their children start school, there are no targets for providing services to children who are one, two or three years old.

Thus, although children in Sweden and in other Nordic nations, including Finland, start formal instructional schooling later than the children do in Australia and other English-speaking countries, they enter high quality ECEC environments earlier. In the Nordic countries, the role of ECEC services is to support families and to meet the foundational developmental needs of young children, including their need to form their identity and feel secure in themselves. This is done in a way which respects the natural learning strategies of young children, which means learning through play, interaction with each other and with the natural world, co-operative activities, and personal investigation. The aim is for children to develop curiosity for, enjoyment in, and confidence about learning; rather than meeting pre-determined requirement levels of knowledge and proficiency.[26]

The fact that a high proportion of Swedish children enter the public space of ECEC services from the age of one means that ECEC workers identify children with learning, behavioural and developmental difficulties, which in Australia are not identified until later. Janson points out that policy-makers in Sweden are very interested in the views of early childhood workers. Those workers see the children much more often than doctors do, which means that they gain considerable knowledge of, and can have a great impact on, the child's development. Many parents take their child to a doctor because of something first noticed by an early childhood worker. In the early years, whereas the parents worry most about physical problems, the early childhood workers worry more about psychological and developmental problems and are very good at identifying those.[27]

---

26   OECD, *Starting Strong II: Early Childhood Education and Care*, pp. 59–61.
27   Janson comments in Scott (ed.), *Changing Children's Chances*, pp. 29–30.

CHAPTER 2

The Australian Early Development Index (AEDI) is an instrument introduced in Australia in 2004 which has assembled nationwide data on the developmental health of all five-year-olds. It covers their physical health and wellbeing, social competence, emotional maturity, language and cognitive skills, communication skills and general knowledge. The AEDI results are available for all local areas and provide a very positive resource to inform action to be taken early to prevent children's problems from becoming entrenched and worsening. They draw on the considerable knowledge which teachers have of children who are in their first year of formal full-time school. Australia's ability to thoroughly identify children's health and developmental needs between the ages of one and four, however, cannot occur until Australia takes steps towards the type of more comprehensive arrangements which characterise Sweden. The immunisations and developmental checks which Australian children have in their first year of life lead to some usage, during the following few years, of maternal and child health services operated by local government councils. These, however, vary considerably between different states and territories, and there is less usage of these services by less socio-economically advantaged families. Thus many Australian two- and three-year-olds do not usually enter another environment where structured health checks are done until they turn four and go into preschool. Australia needs to reduce the considerable gap between newborn babies' access to child health services during their first year of life and the later contact with child health services, which many do not have again until age four. Those arrangements must include having a high level of professionalism available and equitably distributed throughout Australia's ECEC services for children from the age of one.

Associate Professor Sharon Goldfeld is the AEDI research director at The Royal Children's Hospital Centre for Community Child Health in Melbourne. She points out that Australia has made great advances in immunising children. As a result, child health inequalities which exist in Australia – such as lower birth weights for indigenous children and for children in remote locations and from socio-economically disadvantaged backgrounds – do not exist in relation to immunisation. This success in providing universal free child immunisations, and universal health insurance (Medicare), means that, for Australia, according to Goldfeld, it is not unrealistic to aspire to more universal child health arrangements comparable to those which exist in Sweden and the other main Nordic countries.[28]

Australian early childhood expert Professor Deborah Brennan, who has studied Sweden closely, points out that Sweden has a well-resourced ECEC system which is based mainly on publicly provided, tax-financed services and relies little on the operations of the private marketplace, whereas Australia, by contrast, relies very heavily on the private marketplace to deliver childcare services. In Sweden, fees for families who need hours beyond the free minimum services provided are charged at the rate of 3 per cent, 2 per cent, or 1 per cent of combined household income for the first, second and third child respectively. Fees are capped at approximately 1,260 Swedish kronor (SEK) which equals $192 per month for the first child; SEK 840 ($128) for the second child, and SEK 420 ($64) for the third child. The national and municipal governments together pay 90 per

---

28 Sharon Goldfeld, 'The Role of Child Health Systems in Reducing Inequalities' in Scott (ed.), *Changing Children's Chances*, pp. 22–26. See also her comments in other parts of that volume including p. 30.

cent of the cost of all ECEC services, which makes the fees paid by parents to cover the other 10 per cent of ECEC services affordable. In Australia, childcare has expanded rapidly as a for-profit business in the market, which has caused instabilities, serious problems of affordability and has exacerbated inequalities between children. Australia's childcare system is now less marketised than it was in 2008 when the largest for-profit provider, ABC Learning, collapsed and the government assisted moves by the more community-oriented GoodStart to take over the centres which it had operated. However, the more fundamental lessons from that episode about market forces not being appropriate to dominate the realm of ECEC have not been learned.

Professor Brennan is concerned that the bringing together of preschools, or kindergartens as they are known in some states, on the one hand – and childcare centres on the other hand – into integrated ECEC services is much harder in Australia than in Sweden. This is because in Australia, the childcare sector is marketised, whereas early education for three- and four-year-olds is mostly not marketised. Australian policy situates childcare as a commodity to be purchased by consumers; whereas in Sweden children have a social entitlement to ECEC. Further, the federal system in Australia aggravates the difficulties in achieving integrated ECEC. Essentially, Australia's national government focuses on childcare services which meet the needs of working parents, while state governments deliver educationally focused preschool and/or kindergarten programs.

Brennan is further concerned that funding mechanisms, subsidy structures and various eligibility rules exacerbate this division between the types of services provided by each level of government, rather than those services being coherently driven by the needs of parents and families. Moreover, in Australia, with few exceptions, governments do not plan or allocate childcare services. The national government assumes that private, for-profit providers will deliver these services where they are needed and that regulation will ensure desirable outcomes, including quality. Yet the theoretical market liberal assumption that consumers will discipline providers by taking their 'business' (which means their children) elsewhere if services are not of high quality does not hold up well when it comes to ECEC services. Australia is also very different from Sweden in the ongoing tension that it experiences between paying fair wages to educators and carers and keeping fees manageable for parents. For Australia to have a universal and accessible ECEC system, governments will have to take more responsibility for funding fair and appropriate staff wages. Providers face a constant trade-off between paying decent wages to staff and keeping fees affordable for parents. If staff wages go up, then the provider has to have a way of funding those, which will usually be by increasing the fees charged to parents. The national government does help by providing the Child Care Benefit and Child Care Rebate subsidies to those parents who are eligible, which meet a large proportion of the fee costs which those eligible parents incur. Nevertheless, childcare centres continue to debate whether they will pay wage increments to their staff, *or* undertake the necessary refurbishment of a centre. It is unacceptable that these two essential requirements are put in opposition to each other.[29] A shift towards more expanded publicly provided ECEC services in Australia would help achieve goals of greater quality, accessibility

29   The above three paragraphs draw on Deborah Brennan, 'The Importance of High Quality and Accessible Early Childhood Education and Care' in Scott (ed.), *Changing Children's Chances*, pp. 33–36. See also her comments in other parts of that volume.

and affordability: all three of which are too important for any one of them to be forsaken for another.

Australia did take a big step towards higher quality in 2008 when an agreement was made by the Council of Australian Governments (COAG) on a goal that by 2013 every child in Australia, in the year before they start full-time formal schooling, will have access to 15 hours of ECEC services a week, for 40 weeks a year, provided by an early childhood teacher with a four-year university qualification. This agreement recognised the critical importance of investing in the early years as the most effective way to prevent inequalities. It thus added to the AEDI and took a step towards a more integrated approach to the early years in Australia. This followed effective advocacy by the Australian Research Alliance for Children and Youth (ARACY), formed in 2002 at the urging of epidemiology professor and child wellbeing advocate, Fiona Stanley, who was named Australian of the Year in 2003. There has since been some progress to reaching the goal but also significant shortfalls. According to the COAG Reform Council in 2013: 'for States and Territories we can report on, over 90 per cent of those enrolled in preschool attended in 2012. But weekly hours of attendance must rise to meet the 15 hour per week goal "for quality learning".'[30]

More now needs to be done to achieve the initial goals, as well as to realise the full potential of, the early childhood policy initiatives taken so far by Australian governments. A goal that every child in Australia will have access to 15 hours of ECEC services a week is not the same as a guarantee that every child actually will receive those services. Australia still needs to successfully attract qualified workers

---

30   COAG Reform Council, *Education in Australia 2012: Five Years of Performance*, COAG Reform Council, Sydney, 2013, p. 8.

into ECEC positions and retain them. The 15-hours-a-week goal is a starting point from which the next priority steps could be: to increase the hours to 20; and/or commence the arrangements for children earlier such as when they turn three rather than waiting until they turn four years of age; and/or focus on achieving higher quality from age one in particular areas.[31] More resources will particularly need to be provided for families in growing but socio-economically disadvantaged outer suburbs of the major capital cities which have high population growth and high concentrations of young children. Currently, however, even the continuation of the goal for 15 hours a week ECEC is uncertain beyond 2015 unless and until a new COAG agreement is reached.

The support by the Australian Labor Government and the Fair Work Australia industrial tribunal in February 2012 of wage rises for low-paid community services workers was another positive step towards improving the security, recognition and professional career paths for the workforce involved in ECEC, who are nearly all women. Better valuing and recognising the experiences and skills of early childhood workers, valuing attributes like patience, care and empathy, which are central to doing their job well, and paying for those attributes, is now required in Australia.

In September 2009, the ARACY conference issued a communiqué stating that 'Australia must learn from cultures with a positive attitude to children and young people...[and] from public policies that achieve high levels of child wellbeing; adequate support for parents, carers and families; and low levels of child poverty...for example, policies in the Nordic countries'. The conference also outlined a major strategy

---

31   See comments by Deborah Brennan and Sharon Goldfeld in Scott (ed.), *Changing Children's Chances*, pp. 38, 36.

'to set internationally comparable health and wellbeing targets for children and young people for the next 20 years' with 'critical elements of this strategy' to include 'raising Australia's international standing to high levels of child and youth wellbeing, to match the levels achieved by the Nordic countries'.[32]

Sweden, like the other Nordic countries, is consistently ranked as having one of the highest levels of gender equality in the world. It stands well above Australia, which ranks 24th in the world in terms of gender equality.[33] Sweden, like the other Nordic countries, has an explicit focus on gender equality, as well as on children, in its ECEC policies. This is lacking in Australia.[34]

Sweden and the other main Nordic nations' high gender-equality ranking is in part because of women's extensive workforce participation, including in leadership positons. OECD data show Sweden, Denmark and Norway as having the world's highest women's workforce participation rates and Finland has the sixth highest, whereas Australia is the 10th highest. They show women's workforce participation rates in Sweden, Denmark and Norway are above 75 per cent, whereas in Australia the rate is below 70 per cent.[35] Australia's overall employment and workforce participation rates are higher than the OECD average, but they remain below those three Nordic European nations, which consistently feature among the very few with the highest overall employment and workforce participation rates.[36]

32 Communiqué from ARACY conference, Melbourne, 4 September 2009.

33 Ricardo Hausmann, Laura D. Tyson, Yasmina Bekhouche and Saadia Zahidi, *The Global Gender Gap Report 2013*, World Economic Forum, Geneva, 2013, p. 8.

34 Deborah Brennan, 'The Importance of High Quality and Accessible Early Childhood Education and Care', p. 35.

35 Tiffen and Gittins, *How Australia Compares, Second Edition*, Table 4.5.

36 For recent available data, see *OECD Employment Outlook 2013*, Statistical Annex, Tables B, C.

Australia's Productivity Commission report on parental leave, which underpinned the eventual introduction of the basic national paid maternity leave in Australia in 2011, noted evidence that, in the years in which they are most likely to become parents, Australian women's workforce participation rates are much lower than many other OECD countries. The report mentioned data from a Swedish study showing that paid parental leave prompts significantly higher rates of return to work in the long run.[37] It also quoted from another study, among the findings of which is that Australia stands 20th in the rankings of OECD countries for the workforce participation rate of women aged 25 to 44 years old, whereas Sweden is the top-ranked nation.[38] Contrary though it is to orthodox market liberal thinking about the consequences of governments providing benefits in a market-oriented economy, the provision of more paid parental leave actually generates *higher* rates of workforce participation.

Boosting Australia's workforce participation rate to the same rate as Sweden would greatly increase Australia's national productivity, without further work intensification or further *im*balance between work and family for those already in the paid workforce.

It would also significantly cut child poverty. This is because, as social policy analyst Professor Peter Whiteford, points out, Australia has 'one of the highest concentrations of joblessness among families of any OECD country'. In Australia, 'half of the individuals who do not have paid work live in households where there is *nobody* in paid work. By contrast, in Sweden...only a quarter of the individuals

---

37   Productivity Commission, *Paid Parental Leave: Support for Parents with Newborn Children*, Productivity Commission, Canberra, 2009, pp. 5.7–5.8, 5.31, 5.34–5.35.

38   Joanna Abhayaratna and Ralph Lattimore, *Workforce Participation Rates – How Does Australia Compare?*, Staff Working Paper, Productivity Commission, Canberra, 2006, pp. 49, 51.

who do not have paid work live in households where there is nobody in paid work'. Thus, "joblessness is not only a major cause of child poverty, it is also a major cause of inequality in Australia'.[39] Whiteford calculates that reducing the proportion of families in which neither parent works towards the consistently low levels of the Nordic nations could in itself cut income poverty among Australian children by as much as one-third.[40]

The employment orientation of Sweden's 'dual earner' support policy and welfare state is a major reason for Sweden's low rate of child poverty. The OECD emphasises that all countries which have very low rates of child poverty achieve these in part because they have high proportions of parents in paid employment. The high employment rates, including proper forms and standards of part-time work for women, help cut child poverty in Sweden to among the lowest levels in the world. Employment rates for mothers with children whose youngest child is aged three to five are the highest in the world in Sweden at 81.3 per cent.[41]

More than 80 per cent of sole parents in Sweden are also in paid employment, whereas less than 60 per cent of sole parents in Australia are.[42] Among many important points that Peter Whiteford makes in this area of policy is that the employment orientation of the universal welfare states in Sweden and the other Nordic nations means that

---

39 Peter Whiteford, 'The Central Importance of Parental Employment for Reducing Child Poverty in Australia' in Scott (ed.), *Changing Children's Chances*, pp. 47–50 (my emphasis).

40 Peter Whiteford and Willem Adema, *What Works Best in Reducing Child Poverty: A Benefit or Work Strategy?*, OECD Social, Employment and Migration Working Papers, No. 51, Paris, 2007, p. 29.

41 OECD, *Babies and Bosses – Reconciling Work and Family Life: A Synthesis of Findings for OECD Countries*, OECD, Paris, 2007, pp. 16–17.

42 Whiteford, 'The Central Importance of Parental Employment for Reducing Child Poverty in Australia', p. 48.

'their welfare programs both *support and* require people to have jobs'. As he writes: 'in countries with low levels of joblessness such as the Nordic countries, the public policy framework is based on encouraging and facilitating participation in paid work by mothers when their children are still quite young, and also providing the extensive *support* that is sometimes required to achieve this objective'.[43] In Sweden, therefore, sole parents are not just required to enter paid employment, they are supported to enter paid employment. The question is whether Australia gives enough support.

In addition to the extensive paid parental leave, the comprehensive, high quality and affordable public ECEC services and the fact that these services open early to enable parents to drop children off on their way to full-time work, sole parents in Sweden are supported by a suite of employment-assistance programs. These include job-matching, training and other skill-upgrading programs, which are made available to those who need them from an early stage of benefit receipt. Public spending on active labour market measures is comparatively high in Sweden. These supports enable parents on income support to focus on, including to plan for, their workforce re-integration even while they are caring for a young child.[44]

In Australia, the approach to sole parents who are not in paid employment (and whose families are therefore jobless) is to cut their existing meagre benefit payments to try to punitively push them into paid work. The evidence from Sweden's experience is that sole parents, instead, need more support to enter paid work, through the creation of actual job opportunities, expanded provision of

43   Peter Whiteford, *Family Joblessness in Australia: A Paper Commissioned by the Social Inclusion Unit of the Department of the Prime Minister and Cabinet,* Commonwealth of Australia, Canberra, 2009, pp. 26, 59, 61 (my emphasis).

44   OECD, *Babies and Bosses,* pp. 87, 137.

high quality, accessible and affordable childcare, and effective job-training programs tailored to overcome the particular nature of their disadvantage.

In Australia, families which are persistently jobless tend to have very complex, multiple needs. They face many barriers to workforce participation such as domestic violence and homelessness. Their joblessness is usually intergenerational. Of the jobless parents who have been out of paid work for more than a year, 40 per cent have not finished year 10 of school. They thus need to take several steps *before* they can go into paid employment. Inadequacies of local public transport and concerns about neighbourhood safety are two of the biggest problems facing jobless families in disadvantaged areas.[45]

The Spirit Level shows that Sweden, like the other Nordic nations, is among the countries in the world with the lowest rates of teenage pregnancies compared with much higher rates in more unequal countries like Australia.[46] Concern about teenage birth rates being high can come from a moralistic conservative perspective, or it can come from an egalitarian perspective. The egalitarian perspective seeks to ensure that young women are able to meet their needs and to fulfil some of their own important aspirations before having children and also that children are born into circumstances which give them the best possible start in life. Wilkinson and Pickett point out that: 'teenage birth rates are higher in communities that also have high divorce rates, low levels of trust and low social cohesion, high unemployment, poverty and high crime rates...Unequal societies affect teenage child bearing in particular'. In such areas, 'motherhood is a way in which young women in deprived circumstances join adult

---

45   Whiteford comments in Scott (ed.), *Changing Children's Chances*, p. 53.
46   Wilkinson and Pickett, *The Spirit Level*, p. 122.

social networks...supportive networks which help them transcend the social stigma of their lives' which have been shaped by the inequalities they have experienced from an early age.[47]

Staffan Janson emphasises that parents in neighbourhoods of high poverty and unemployment, with weak community infrastructure, and with poorly planned and maintained housing, are under more financial pressure and have higher rates of alcohol and drug abuse, along with other risk factors for child abuse. Children in these areas have less faith in the future and are at increased risk of future unemployment. What needs to be done therefore is to renovate the areas, to strengthen services and security and to strengthen neighbour co-operation, he argues.[48]

Australia and other English-speaking countries cannot and will not move suddenly from a targeted welfare state to a universal welfare state such as in Sweden and the other main Nordic nations. However, there have recently been some place-based initiatives in Australia which seek to respond to jobless families' characteristics of disadvantage and to support members of those families to make the transition into paid work. A high policy priority should be to adjust and to effectively build on those.

The initiatives include the Communities for Children program, a prevention and early intervention initiative implemented in 45 particular disadvantaged communities around Australia since 2004. It forms partnerships of community organisations to improve service coordination and collaboration in meeting the needs of children under the age of five and their families. Evaluations of this initiative found

47   Ibid. pp. 121, 125, 128.
48   Staffan Janson, 'An Overview of Nordic Policy for Children: Lessons for Australia on How to Reduce Inequalities', pp. 20–21.

significant improvements in outcomes for participating children, families and communities. These included improved receptive vocabulary and verbal skills in children from low-income households or where mothers had year 10 school education or less, and less hostile and harsh parenting practices. There have been improvements as a result of the program, too, in terms of more children living in households where at least one parent is employed. More 'hard to reach' families have evidently been equally likely to benefit from this program, which has: reduced service gaps; increased the prevention of problems likely to lead to the need for intervention by child protection services; and increased the engagement of families.[49]

The *Building Australia's Future Workforce* package in Australia's 2011 national budget extended the Communities for Children program and introduced new measures to tackle geographical disadvantage. A 'Supporting Jobless Families' initiative includes a trial from January 2012, in ten locations around Australia, which requires parents in families where neither is in paid work to make participation plans and offers them support to help boost skills they need and to prepare their children to be ready for school. These trial initiatives include interviews with parents when the youngest child is aged one, two and three, which focus on child health, development and wellbeing, and which make sure parents have access to necessary support services. After the youngest child turns four, parents attend a workshop to undertake activities to prepare for returning to work and for meeting the participation requirements expected of them once their child reaches school age.

---

49   COAG, *Investing in the Early Years – A National Early Childhood Development Strategy: An Initiative of the Council of Australian Governments*, Commonwealth of Australia, Canberra, 2009, p. 11.

These trials have some positive elements, and data from them will be useful to inform future initiatives. However, they are limited in number and coverage and, in addition to their emphasis on requirements more than support, there is concern about the quality of that support which is provided. Nevertheless, further, adjusted place-based initiatives could be part of helping to cut child poverty in Australia towards the low levels of Sweden and the other main Nordic nations.

Jobless families in Australia include many (and will soon swell in number to include many more) parents who are former manufacturing workers, middle-aged and older, concentrated in particular geographic areas. The AEDI reveals problems which children have in particular geographic concentrations. It thus opens up the possibilities for expanded place-based measures, for a geographical approach to overcome particular neighbourhoods' disadvantage by tackling concentrations of joblessness. Greater support for – as well as requirement of – the people in those geographic areas which the AEDI and other data show as disadvantaged will be the best way to approach future place-based interventions in those areas. To overcome particular neighbourhoods' disadvantage, including joblessness, and to build on the beginnings which Australian governments have made, it will be beneficial for details of practically successful, local, multi-faceted, child health, parenting and employment programs in Sweden to be obtained. These can inform the introduction and trial of a new place-based approach, one which is 'very purposeful and experimental',[50] in particular locations in Australia which the AEDI and other data identify as disadvantaged. More extensive place-based initiatives for job pathways, skills development and support services

---

50   Sharon Goldfeld's words in Scott (ed.), *Changing Children's Chances*, p. 55.

for families, including sole parents, in places of high joblessness should be pursued in Australia to overcome obstacles to the take-up and retention of paid work by those families.

There is a strong desire in Australia for better work/life balance to enable work to be manageably combined with caring for children. Because of the encroachments by new technology, such as the latest mobile phone devices, emails can be sent and viewed at any time, which makes it harder now to put boundaries around working life. Many parents regret the fact they are not able to spend more time with their children, nor give their children their full attention when they are with them, due to work worries and distractions seeping into that time. At least one-quarter of Australian workers are experiencing work pressures which negatively interfere with their lives. Women in full-time work, in particular, are experiencing the pressure of balancing paid work with their other commitments. Nearly seven out of ten full-time working women 'often or almost always feel rushed and pressed for time'. Couples with children most want to reduce their hours of work. The weak provisions since 2010 whereby workers can request more flexible working hours are very little known and not effectively used, particularly among mothers of preschool children.[51] By contrast, parents in Sweden are legally entitled to considerably reduce their working hours until their children turn eight. For many, this is a powerful and absolutely crucial entitlement for their wellbeing and for their children's wellbeing.

The OECD finds that Australia is one of a small number of countries in which long hours, including for women, are most common, whereas – in addition to their substantial paid parental

---

51   The data in this paragraph draw on Skinner, Hutchinson and Pocock, *The Big Squeeze*, 2013, pp. 3, 7, 11, 36–37, 71.

leave, public ECEC and other support – parents in Sweden and the other main Nordic countries have working weeks shorter than the OECD average.[52] The fact that Sweden and the other main Nordic nations' weekly working hours are considerably less than Australia's enables parents there to pick up their children after work from ECEC facilities without time pressures. Australia will probably move to make childcare centres' hours more flexible to suit Australia's long working hours. It would be better to make the working hours shorter, and more compatible with family life, including more compatible with parents' picking up of children from ECEC facilities before the evening meal.

The crumbling of the boundaries between work and home on the magnitude that is occurring in Australia is leading to considerable and increasing unpaid work. More than three million workers in Australia may now be losing sleep because of work stress. 'The current labour environment is contributing to high levels of stress and anxiety; sleep loss and depression for many Australians. This has adverse effects on their health, family life and relationships' and, ironically, is actually an impediment to reaching 'the national goal for greater economic productivity'.[53] Australia therefore needs to again discuss further regulation of the labour market, particularly regulation of working hours, in order to achieve more family-friendliness, more child-friendliness and better work/life balance in employment arrangements.

Policy-makers in Australia should value children more highly, place their needs at the centre of policy and then make corresponding

---

52   OECD, *Babies and Bosses*, pp. 174, 171.

53   Prue Cameron and Richard Denniss, *Hard to Get a Break? Hours, Leave and Barriers to Re-entering the Australian Workforce*, The Australia Institute, Canberra, 2013, p. 1.

changes in policy. The Australian people will support such policy change if they are shown the clear evidence of its social and economic benefits. Values can be changed through policies as occurred with Swedish attitudes to physical violence against children. Many Australians' high valuing of children is not adequately expressed in current policies in Australia. One country can learn and change from the comparative study of another country's positive values and policies.

The Nordic nations' productivity-oriented cultures are based on the premises that work is good, that work should be enjoyable and that work should be able to be balanced throughout one's life with other major transitions in life, of which the arrival and the raising of children is obviously one.

Sweden, like the other main Nordic nations, has achieved its policy successes for children through steady incremental effort over many decades. Australia has recently started to develop more positive policies for children based on clear international evidence. Australia should continue to do so, drawing on, and learning in particular from Sweden's strong investment in public, high quality ECEC services, provision of substantial paid parental leave and effective regulation of working hours. These policies will promote secure jobs suitable for work/family balance, boost women's labour force participation and reduce joblessness among families with children.

Under the Abbott Government, there is concern that Australia's tentative progress in improving the quality of ECEC will be reversed to save costs. Yet Australia spends just one-quarter of what Sweden spends, and half the OECD average on ECEC.[54] More, rather than

---

54 OECD, *Starting Strong II: Early Childhood Education and Care*, p. 105.

less, investment in early childhood programs must now be made if child poverty in Australia is to be reduced.

The Abbott Government set up a new Productivity Commission enquiry into ECEC but this was limited from the outset by the fact that any changes had to be within existing funding parameters. Although the enquiry was asked to consider approaches taken overseas which might be suitable to try in Australia, this consideration was directed towards following New Zealand's precedent of subsidising the engagement of in-home 'nannies' to provide childcare; rather than towards considering the much more successful policy approach for children taken by Sweden and the other main Nordic nations.

The conundrum which Tony Abbott's Right-of-centre government has created for the ALP, by his out-of-character move to introduce more substantial paid parental leave, has not been responded to well by Labor, which has condemned the plan as 'middle-class welfare'. Substantial paid parental leave should instead be regarded as a workplace right, as the Swedish Social Democratic Party has regarded it for 40 years. The ALP's overblown rhetoric condemning more substantial parental leave as 'handouts to millionaires' contradicts its own – and correct – policy of not means-testing Child Care Rebates, sick leave, annual leave, long-service leave, and universal health insurance (Medicare). The Abbott Government's policy will indeed benefit higher income earners, among others: but all more universalist arrangements do. The principles of universalism need to be supported here, irrespective of who initiated the policy, and those principles equally need to be supported against any actions which might be taken which would erode Medicare and further reduce Australia's already minimal welfare state. If the government proposes to extend the Child Care Rebate to – or create new subsidies for – the engagement of 'nannies' in the home, then this will not bring the same valuable social learning benefits of the early mixing with other children which occurs in ECEC facilities. If the more expansive paid parental leave scheme is paid for by ECEC cuts or by an increase in the regressive GST, then it is those cuts, and the using of those measures as the source of funding, which should be opposed, rather than the expanded paid parental leave scheme itself.

Despite its low level of child poverty, and minimal health differences between indigenous and non-indigenous children, reports prepared by Malmö University's Professor Tapio Salonen, for Save the Children Sweden, show that children of immigrant families within Sweden have significantly higher rates of poverty than children from Swedish backgrounds.[55] Overcoming this inequality must now be part of Sweden meeting its more general challenge for more successful 'integration' of immigrants, and part of building on the outstanding, world-leading role it has taken for children.

---

55   Tapio Salonen, *Barnfattigdom i Sverige*, Rädda Barnen, Stockholm, Årsrapport, 2013, p. 20.

Chapter 3

A STUNNING SUCCESS
IN SCHOOLS:
FINLAND
SINCE THE 1990S

In a similar way to how early childhood workers are valued in Sweden, school teachers in general are valued in Finland. Proper valuing of the profession of teaching is one important explanation for Finland's very high standings in the Program for International Student Assessment (PISA) results. These assessments have been conducted, and the results released, every three years since 2000. Finland's approach to school education has attracted considerable international interest since that nation's exceptional results in the PISA assessments began to be reported from the early 21st century.

Finland has raised the social status of its teaching profession to a very high level through actions including requirement of a research-based master's degree, involving at least five years of rigorous study, to enter the profession. The degree culminates with the prospective Finnish teachers formulating an educational question into which to enquire, searching for information on this question, then developing the results into a coherent analysis in a written thesis. This helps them to gain not only deep knowledge of recent research advances in the specific subjects which they will teach but also deep knowledge of research advances in teaching and learning in general.[1] In Finland, there is very strict quality control of entry to teacher education degrees. Only about one in ten of the applicants to be teachers are accepted. The judgements about whether they are accepted are determined by their personality and commitment as well as by their academic ability. 'Teacher candidates are selected, in part, according to their capacity to convey their belief in the core mission of public education in Finland'. This mission 'is deeply humanistic as well as civic and economic'.[2] Finns who choose to go into the teaching profession are thus very passionate about making a difference to young people's lives and to shaping those young people's futures. They do not see teaching as just a job, which is a substitute for doing something else which was preferred.

However, according to the Finnish educational expert who is best-known in the English-speaking world, Dr Pasi Sahlberg, it is not enough to improve teacher education and raise student admission requirements. Finnish experience indicates that it is even more important to provide a professional working environment for teachers in schools. Sahlberg considers that, in explaining Finland's educational achievements, 'one factor trumps all others: the daily contributions of excellent teachers'. The environment in which those teachers work must ensure dignity for those who enter the profession to sustain their idealism for teaching as a life-long career, he argues. Achieving a balance in teachers' work between classroom teaching and collaboration with other professionals in schools is essential to

1   Hannele Niemi, 'The Societal Factors Contributing to Education and Schooling in Finland' in Hannele Niemi, Auli Toom and Arto Kallioniemi (eds.), *Miracle of Education: The Principles and Practices of Teaching and Learning in Finnish Schools*, Sense Publishers, Rotterdam, 2012, pp. 32–33.

2   Andreas Schleicher, *Building a High-Quality Teaching Profession: Lessons from around the World*, OECD, Paris, 2011, p. 17.

attract talented people to become school teachers. This is not done by the imposition of performance-based pay for individual teachers, which tends to destroy teamwork. Instead, there has been systematic development of 'respectful and interesting' working conditions for teachers and leaders in Finnish schools. This includes giving teachers freedom for their own creative initiative to bloom.[3] By contrast, in Australia, schoolteachers are not given the level of professional respect which they deserve. On the contrary, they are very frequently targets of harsh and unjustified criticism.

Australia needs to consolidate arrangements for entry to the teaching profession towards a new five-year requirement, rather than the current typical four-year requirement, to qualify to become a school teacher. As well as raising entry standards, there is a pressing need for more opportunities for the ongoing professional development of school teachers in Australia. Australian Education Union Federal Secretary Susan Hopgood, based on her visits to Finland and close contact with her counterparts there, has observed how, in Finland, school teachers 'are encouraged to be active learners throughout their career'. In Australia, by contrast, there are no systematic programs or resources to support this. 'In Finland, they see it as a core part of teachers' work, that you constantly upgrade your skills and knowledge, and you do that collectively. There is a very collegial approach to that in schools: teachers working together. I gained the impression that they are very happy to be in and out of each other's classrooms,' she says.[4]

---

3   Pasi Sahlberg, *Finnish Lessons: What Can the World Learn from Educational Change in Finland?*, Teachers College Press, Columbia University, New York, 2011, pp. 70, 12, 7, 94.
4   Interview with Susan Hopgood, Federal Secretary, Australian Education Union.

CHAPTER 3

In Finland, schools are also very well-designed and resourced, with excellent, well-maintained facilities, which makes them stimulating and rewarding places in which to work. There may not be in Finnish schools the heights of luxury available in some of the most wealthy, fee-charging private schools in Australia. However, most teachers in Finnish schools are working in better – including better-maintained – facilities than are most Australian school teachers. The principal of Cygnaeus Upper Secondary School in the central Finnish city of Jyväskylä, Ari Pokka, advises that 'normally in Finland, if you make a new school or renew an older school, the teachers and principals have a lot of say in what the school will look like, what the equipment is, what the architecture style is'. He adds that the teachers also work with the people who actually construct the buildings. For example, in current plans for his school's new building, he and his colleagues are arranging for it to be able to practically demonstrate the use of solar power during chemistry lessons. Pokka emphasises that 'in Finnish schools, not only the school cultures are different because of the autonomy of the school but also…the school buildings including the classrooms reflect how much teachers have influenced the things inside. The pedagogical approach, the way you work with the kids, is also [about] how you plan your environment and use it in your learning and teaching'.[5] It is interesting to note the similarities between these points and the Norwegian and Swedish work-design initiatives which attracted Australian interest from the 1960s, as was discussed in Chapter 1.

Finland does not spend markedly more on education than Australia. National expenditure on education as a proportion of Gross

5   Interview with Ari Pokka, Immediate Past President of the Finnish Association of Principals (SUREFIRE) and president-elect of the International Confederation of Principals (ICP).

Domestic Product in Australia is 6.1 per cent, which is below the OECD average of 6.3 per cent. Finland spends 6.5 per cent. These are not very significant differences. However, of the various nations' expenditures on education, in Australia *public* expenditure makes up only 75 per cent, whereas in the OECD, on average, *public* expenditure makes up more than 85 per cent; while in Finland, *public* expenditure makes up more than 98 per cent.[6] These are very significant differences. Most importantly, Finland is starkly distinct from Australia in that *it does not allow private schools to charge fees.* Australia, meanwhile, is starkly distinct from nearly every other country in the OECD in the large sums of government money which go to private schools, many of which charge very high fees for students. Australia has a very divided school education system with many very wealthy private schools to which government gives money, for historical political reasons. Many Australians who in principle want to send their child to the local government school decide that in practice, however, they need to ensure the best poss- ible education for their individual child, so they pay money, which may be difficult for them to afford, to send that child to a private school. So the public school system becomes more and more resid- ual. Finland by contrast sustains a very strong comprehensive and high quality public school system by making it illegal for private schools to charge fees there.

The typical salary level of Finnish school teachers is similar to Australian school teachers.[7] Susan Hopgood believes that, in Fin- land, 'young people don't go into teaching because of the salaries,

6   All figures computed from OECD, *Education at a Glance 2013*, OECD, Paris, 2013, p. 193.
7   OECD, *OECD Education at a Glance 2012*, OECD, Paris, 2012, pp. 294–316.

they go into teaching because it is a highly regarded profession in which they are interested'. But there is also the fact that as teachers 'their salaries are comparable to similar occupations and professions in Finland'.[8] This reflects Finland's general comparative equality as a nation. It contrasts with the gap which has opened up between the salaries of teachers, and other professional occupations in Australia, as identified by Australia's Productivity Commission in 2012.[9]

A fundamental reason for the Finns' notable educational success is their egalitarian approach to the public funding of schools. The foundations for Finland's stunning success since the 1990s, as demonstrated by PISA results, were laid by institutional reforms to schools undertaken from the 1970s. In that decade in Finland, the comprehensive school (*peruskoulu*) was introduced. It merged existing grammar schools, civic schools, and primary schools into nine-year duration schools in every local area, which all young people who live in that particular area attend. There was a strong campaign against the creation of comprehensive schools in Finland by some private sector employers and the ideological Right, who wanted there to be many private, fee-charging schools instead.[10] So today's Finnish egalitarian education approach, which has proved so successful, did not just happen. On the contrary, it had to be fought for politically. One of the 22 members of a major study tour undertaken by Australian school principals of Finland in 2012, Frank Sal, noted that in Finland now 'parents are bemused when asked whether they would consider not sending their child to the local community [public]

---

8   Hopgood interview.
9   Productivity Commission, *Schools Workforce*, Research Report, Productivity Commission, Canberra, 2012, p. 57.
10 Sahlberg, *Finnish Lessons*, pp. 128, 109, 21, 121, 124, 126, 127, 135.

school'. All schools there are well-regarded, and parents do not have the option to buy access for their children into a perceived superior school outside their local area.[11]

Out-of-school factors, including parents' occupations and the home environment, explain much of the variation in school students' achievements in all countries. Nevertheless, schools, including teachers, can make a difference to the remaining variations in achievement. One positive way that schools can do this is by bringing together students from a mix of socio-economic backgrounds.

Various OECD reports arising from the PISA results have identified some startling facts and stark messages from Finland's success for English-speaking countries. At the 2009 PISA, for example, variation in reading performance *between* schools was less than 10 per cent in Finland, compared with more than 30 per cent in Australia. The variation in reading performance which was explained by the effect of students' and schools' socio-economic background was less than 30 per cent in Finland, but more than 70 per cent in Australia.[12] Variation in mathematics performance between schools at the 2012 PISA, meanwhile, was just over 6 per cent in Finland compared with more than 30 per cent in Australia.[13]

These outcomes reflect the fact that the Australian education system is one of the most highly segregated along socio-economic lines in the OECD. Only 20 per cent of the bottom socio-economic quarter attend private schools in Australia compared with 60 per cent of the

11 Frank Sal, 'Observations and Reflections from Finland Learnings', typescript document, 2012. Frank is President of the Victorian Association of State Secondary Principals.

12 OECD, *PISA 2009 Results: Overcoming Social Background: Equity in Learning Opportunities and Outcomes*, OECD, Paris, 2010, pp. 85, 89.

13 OECD, *PISA 2012 Results: Excellence through Equity: Giving Every Student the Chance to Succeed*, OECD, Paris, 2013, p. 47 (Figure II.2.7).

top socio-economic quarter. Nearly 60 per cent of disadvantaged students in Australia attend disadvantaged schools, whereas less than 10 per cent attend advantaged schools.[14] Students at well-resourced private schools, or at government schools in high socio-economic areas in Australia, gain lifelong benefits and advantages which are denied to most young Australians.

A crucial part of the socio-economic inequalities between Australian schools is the way in which vocational education continues to be situated as second-rate. Finland, by contrast, has coherent vocational educational opportunities in upper secondary education which are available in an equitable way.

Dr Stephen Lamb, then a research fellow (and now a professor) in The University of Melbourne's Graduate School of Education, travelled in 2008 to study school-based vocational education and training in many countries. His research showed that nations with separate occupationally structured vocational education programs, such as Finland, have very high rates of school completion, well above the OECD average, and the lowest numbers of students who leave school without a qualification. Their school-based courses last for two to four years, and some provide avenues to university. By contrast, Australia has a system similar to America in which students can choose from a menu of vocational education subjects or units as part of the general upper secondary school curriculum. Students can choose to do none, or as many, of the vocational education subjects as they wish, leading to varying levels of intensity of vocational study in each school, state and territory. Vocational education systems in which students choose a whole course of study, rather than a set of subject

---

14   OECD, *Equity and Quality in Education: Supporting Disadvantaged Students and Schools*, OECD, Paris, 2012, p. 66 (Figure 2.2) and p. 109 (Figure 3.4).

or unit options, have higher standards of learning and achievement, according to PISA results. Only 14 per cent of Australian students were at that time doing mainly vocational education courses.[15] The proportion of students in upper secondary schools in Finland who are enrolled in full vocational education courses is currently above 40 per cent.[16]

Lamb later elaborated on this research, writing that the 'completion of basic education [which means the nine year comprehensive school] in Finland leads to a choice in upper secondary school between general education or a vocational program. Both alternatives last three years and completion of the studies provides eligibility to apply for higher education...Finland during the 1980s and 1990s... implemented a number of educational reforms to upper secondary program provision focusing largely on vocational education as a means of encouraging students to stay in school'. It is where 'separate vocational education programs are offered in upper secondary education, but these programs retain links with academic and general education and keep open avenues to higher education', of which 'examples are provided in several Nordic countries, in[cluding]... Finland' that 'the highest attainment levels' are reached. Crucially, this is because these countries 'permit movement between such programs and academic or general education'.[17]

15   Caroline Milburn, 'Trades Face "Class" Divide', *The Age*, Melbourne, 2 March 2009. For further details, see Stephen Lamb, 'Successful Provision of VET in Schools: Overseas Approaches, *VOCAL: The Australian Journal of Vocational Education and Training in School*, Vol. 7, 2008–2009, pp. 117–121.

16   Finnish National Board of Education information at http://www.oph.fi/english/ education_system/upper_secondary_education_and_training.

17   Stephen Lamb, 'Pathways to School Completion: An International Comparison' in Stephen Lamb, Eifred Markussen, Richard Teese, Nina Sandberg and John Polesel (eds.), *School Dropout and Completion: International Comparative Studies in Theory and Policy*, Springer, Dordrecht, 2010, pp. 55, 69, 60–61.

Another member of the 2012 Australian school principals' study tour of Finland was Tim Blunt, the principal of Sunshine College, in the heart of Melbourne's socio-economically disadvantaged western suburbs. He was similarly impressed by how, in Finland, 'students enter either vocational upper secondary schools, academic upper secondaries or others specialising in [areas such as] music, language or sport'. Different upper secondary Finnish schools specialise in natural sciences or mathematics. Blunt also observed how 'all upper secondaries are well resourced and lead on to university or polytechnic colleges, with students able to switch between the two streams if they want to change course'. Further, 'in some municipalities, vocational colleges are harder to get into than the more mainstream academic schools'. 'If you have agreement that there needs to be courses for kids' individual talents then you can't neglect the talents of kids who want to be tradespeople,' Blunt says. He regards it as unfortunate that Australia does not give the same support for young people who want to follow that path. 'We want to get to the level that we witnessed in Finland where year 10 students' aspire to go into trades and 'it's not just seen as somewhere to end up because you're not good at school'. Blunt has thus set up a similar pathway for year 10 students at Sunshine College. In 2008, in conjunction with Victoria University (which is also in Melbourne's western suburbs), the school established what is now the Harvester Technical College on one of its campuses. The arrangement allows more than 150 students to stay at the school and to study Technical and Further Education (TAFE) courses delivered by staff from the school as well as from the university and other tertiary providers as they progress through years 10, 11 and 12. According to Blunt, 'some young kids find it too hard to go directly to TAFE and start a course on their own. They end up dropping out. So we're trying to do this on campus with the security of the school environment to support them'.[18]

The Sunshine College initiative has attracted hundreds of young people from other schools, including non-government schools, which were not fulfilling the interest in vocational learning which those young people have: including into manual trades such as plumbing, electrical, carpentry and engineering. This is a major achievement given the failure by successive national governments in Australia to follow through on rhetoric to systematically support vocational education, as a genuine, equal but different option to general education for students in years 10, 11 and 12. For the success of this initiative to become more widespread in Australia, governments will now need to follow through and provide systematic support for vocational education. 'The thing that I noticed in Finland', Blunt says, was that 'the facilities and the equipment were equivalent to a TAFE, they were just fantastic. I couldn't believe I was standing in a secondary school looking at the equipment'.[19]

I had a similar reaction myself when I went into the Vehicle Technology teaching area of Jyväskylä College, a vocational upper secondary school in the central Finnish city. There I saw many full motor vehicles on the floor of a secondary classroom premises where, each year, approximately 200 students in years 10, 11 and 12, who choose to focus on Vehicle Technology, become licensed motor mechanics as part of gaining their vocational upper secondary

---

18 Caroline Milburn, 'With an Eye on the Finnish Line', *The Age*, Melbourne, 4 June 2012; interview with Tim Blunt.

19 Blunt interview. The study tour was by Australian primary and secondary school principals of government schools: members of the Victorian Principals' Association, which covers primary school principals, and the Victorian Association of State Secondary Principals.

school qualification. During year 10, they acquire basic skills in servicing cars, including oil changes. In year 11 they learn to repair both passenger vehicles and heavy-duty trucks, including checking brakes and undertaking wheel alignments. In year 12 they focus on electronics. One of the projects on which the students had worked was the creation of a fully functioning racing car from a stripped-down old vehicle. The students, with their teachers, also run an actual automotive repair shop from the school, used by paying local customers, as part of developing their technical and business skills. The services which the automotive repair shop offer include the changing over of an entire car motor. Meanwhile, as part of studying Logistics, these students learn to safely operate fork-lifts to transport vehicle wheels into warehouse storage. The vocational upper second-ary qualification at Jyväskylä College emphasises on-the-job learning and entrepreneurship studies. There is also a substantial general studies component including languages, mathematics, physics and chemistry, health education, art and culture.[20]

Finland's extensive government investment in the equipment for the vocational schools helps boost their attractiveness as an option. It is based, first, on the belief that there is a good living to be gained from hands-on manual trades for young people who have talents for them. It is based, second, on the belief that young people with such talents should not be pushed onto different pathways which means that they lose interest in upper secondary education. This does not mean that Finland has solved all the challenges of keeping all young people engaged with formal schooling. There was much

---

20   My 2014 visit to the staff and facilities of Jyväskylä College was kindly coordinated, and detailed materials provided to me, by Aino Malin, International Affairs Manager of the municipality-owned Jyväskylä Educational Consortium.

attention being given by several policy makers whom I spoke to there about how girls are increasingly doing better than boys in academic learning.[21] There was similar attention being given to the need for schools to further adapt their traditional methods of teaching to the realities of how young people today spend so much non-school time with electronic devices.

Finland, however, is much better placed than most nations to meet these challenges. An additional reason for this is that there is a comprehensive system of careers advice for Finnish school students which commences in year 7 and intensifies in year 8 as students prepare to make choices for specialisation in upper secondary education. There is assistance for students to make decisions about their future studies and to ensure that, whatever choices they do make, they are not left without positive future options. For decades, the *Ammattistartti* program has assisted those who have completed the nine-year comprehensive school and who have not yet made a decision about their career choice. It enables them to try out various fields of upper secondary vocational education and training, such as construction, or metalwork and machinery, for a few months *before* making a final decision. This program also provides support to improve their study skills and to expand their knowledge base.[22]

Stephen Lamb's research found that 'in Finland...fewer than 10 per cent of 20- to 24-year-olds are without an upper secondary qualification or not in education and training. Furthermore...[Finland has] comparatively high rates of graduation from general and academic pathways and strong entry rates into higher education...[which

---

21   For example, in my interview with Ritva Semi, Special Adviser, OAJ (the Trade Union of Education in Finland).

22   See the Finnish National Board of Education's publication 'Preparatory Instruction and Guidance' downloadable from http://www.oph.fi/english/publications/brochures.

are] 20 per cent...above the OECD average'. When he compares the proportions of students who leave school without gaining a qualification, he finds that in Australia, 'the dropout rate is about 30 per cent...[whereas] in...Finland, it is about 10 per cent'.[23] The fact that socio-economic inequalities between schools undermine overall national education performance can be clearly seen in further comparisons of Australian and Finnish outcomes. Nearly 30 per cent of Australians between the age of 25 and 64 have not attained a senior school certificate, whereas less than 20 per cent have not done so in Finland.[24] The proportion of 15-year-olds in Australia who failed to achieve a baseline level of reading proficiency in 2009 was nearly twice as high as in Finland.[25] In the 2012 PISA results, Australia continued to be outperformed by Finland in mathematical, scientific and reading literacy.[26]

When the Rudd Labor Government was elected in Australia in 2007, it promised an 'education revolution'. Some steps taken were positive, such as directing large sums of money to government primary schools in Australia, which had long been suffering from dilapidated physical conditions and had frequently missed out on refurbishment funds. However, more substantial amounts of money were needed to rectify decades of neglect and of relative funding decline for government schools as distinct from wealthy private schools.

---

23   Lamb, 'Pathways to School Completion', pp. 61, 63.

24   OECD, *Equity and Quality in Education: Supporting Disadvantaged Students and Schools*, 2012, p. 19 (Figure 1.4).

25   OECD, *PISA 2009 Results: Learning Trends: Changes in Student Performance Since 2000*, OECD, Paris, 2010, pp. 42, 43.

26   Sue Thomson, Lisa De Bortoli and Sarah Buckley, *PISA 2012: How Australia Measures Up: The PISA 2012 Assessment of Students' Mathematical, Scientific and Reading Literacy*, Australian Council for Educational Research, Melbourne, 2013, pp. xiii, xiv, ix, xi.

Education Professor Bob Lingard pointed out that when the Australian Labor Government elected in 2007 looked overseas for policy ideas, it looked too singularly at ideas to enforce educational 'accountability' 'from England and the USA, specifically New York City'. This was despite the fact that 'accountability and testing reforms there...[had] been subject to devastating criticisms'. Lingard questioned why these Anglo-American nations remained 'the "reference societies", when...the creation of a global space of measurement of national schooling systems has constituted new and significant reference societies such as Finland'. He also expressed concern that the Rudd Government's so-called education revolution was a contradictory mix of neo-liberal and social democratic aspirations.[27]

One neo-liberal element in the Australian Labor Government's education policy was its insistence on the National Assessment Program – Literacy and Numeracy (NAPLAN) tests in years 3, 5, 7 and 9 across Australia. Another was the 'My School' website rankings. These elements of policy are neo-liberal because they promote the compilation of competitive 'league tables' which are insensitive to the socio-economic inequalities between schools. Publication of those 'league tables', in turn, leads to unfair criticism of the teachers in those schools who work, with great dedication and ability, to overcome the disadvantages which students bring with them when they enter those schools.

NAPLAN tests are an example of the external, standardised, high-stakes national tests which cause much unnecessary and unhelpful anxiety, and even fear, among school students, yet bring little or no educational benefit. Such assessments lead to teaching in order

27 Bob Lingard, 'Policy Borrowing, Policy Learning: Testing Times in Australian Schooling', *Critical Studies in Education*, Vol. 51, No. 2, 2010, pp. 143–144, 132.

to meet particular test requirements, rather than to teaching for the purpose that students learn. Putting a lot of pressure on young people to perform in narrowly confined tests is a very different thing from encouraging them to learn in a way which prepares them well for life's challenges. Such tests provide a clear example of how 'inequality increases evaluation anxieties' as has been discussed by Wilkinson and Pickett in *The Spirit Level*.[28] No such tests exist in Finland.

That is, there are no external standardised high-stakes tests in Finnish comprehensive schools. Assessment of student learning in Finland is, instead, based on teacher-created tests at the school level. Normally, Finnish pupils are not assessed using any numerical grades at all that enable a direct comparison of pupils with one another before year 5 or year 6. Only descriptive assessments and feedback are employed then. In Finland, assessment is conducted according to the principle that 'if you want to increase curiosity' you must 'allow questioning'; and that 'to strengthen learners' self-confidence and learning motivation', it is important to 'give constructive and honest feedback' and to 'never humiliate or put down a learner'. As well, Finland is now seeking to further move 'from assessment of learning towards assessment for learning and assessment as learning'. It emphasises learning at an 'unhurried pace', amid 'peace' and the 'importance of self-reflection' by 'individuals and the whole school community'.[29]

The visiting Australian principals in 2012 commented that 'the Finns want to see what the student knows', rather than 'how much they can regurgitate in a tight three-hour exam like here'.[30] Sahlberg

---

28   Wilkinson and Pickett, *The Spirit Level*, pp. 43–44.

29   Irmelí Halinen, 'Curriculum Reform in Finland' at http://www.oph.fi/download/151294_ops2016_curriculum_reform_in_finland.pdf.

30   Australian School Principals' Report of their 2012 study tour of Finland, typescript document.

writes that 'thematic assessments, reflective self-evaluations, and emphasis on creative learning have established a culture of mutual trust and respect within the Finnish education system' and that teachers there use 'a mix of diagnostic, formative, performance and summative assessments'.[31]

The Australian Literacy Educators' Association advised a 2014 cross-party Senate committee that 'while NAPLAN is intended to be a diagnostic test it cannot, by virtue of the tests themselves, provide the same specific diagnostic outcomes as formative assessment'. Formative assessments 'provide students with specific feedback about the qualities of their work with advice on how it can be improved to build the resilience of students and support a classroom culture of successful learning'.[32]

Although there is not external, standardised, high-stakes national competitive testing in Finland, Frank Sal did note more frequent *classroom* testing there than in Australia.[33] Numerical grades are used after years 5 or 6. Further, in Finland, selection of students for upper secondary school is based on the grades which the individual students achieve for the theoretical subjects in the basic education certificate attained at year 9.[34] Year 9 is an important year for students to reach the standards which they need in order to go to the upper secondary school which has the specialisation(s) of their choice. A national matriculation examination is held at the end of general upper secondary education (i.e. in year 12, for those who do

---

31 Sahlberg, *Finnish Lessons*, pp. 125, 126.
32 The Senate Education and Employment Committee, *Effectiveness of the National Assessment Program – Literacy and Numeracy Final Report*, Australian Parliament, Canberra, March 2014, p. 10.
33 Interview with Frank Sal.
34 Finnish National Board of Education information at http://www.oph.fi/english/ education_system/upper_secondary_education_and_training.

not choose vocational upper secondary education). This, however, is the only national examination which any Finnish school students sit.

Finland's approach to school education does not involve a centralised bureaucracy. Its approach supports local autonomy – but not in the sense of schools' funding levels being determined by how entrepreneurial they are in raising money from private sources. Instead, the Finnish education system supports autonomy in the sense of trusting teachers to adapt, including to add to, the broadly agreed national core curriculum framework. The system trusts teachers to use their professional skills and judgements, and to draw on their close knowledge of their own students in order to meet those particular students' needs, in their own classroom situations, in the best possible way.

Finland's national core curriculum is reviewed every ten years. The review is an exhaustive, four-year consultative process, which starts with open-minded seminars and discussions. It then proceeds to develop objectives and core contents, guidelines for assessment, principles about the provision of support and regulations to ensure student welfare. The process involves numerous inter-disciplinary working groups. It allows major input by any interested stakeholders including individual parents, universities, municipalities and employers. The current process for the adoption of a new national core curriculum to take effect in Finland from 2016 to 2017 asks searching questions about the types of competencies which will be needed for the future. It draws on the findings of recent projects concerning: intensified and special support, student welfare service structures, guidance counselling, multiculturalism and language teaching. Principles in the curriculum review process include: promoting equality, particularly between men and women; entrepreneurship and skills for working life; facilitating democracy, empowerment and influence; and enhancing social skills. Objectives of the review include more participatory, physically active, creative and linguistically enriched schools; and more integrated teaching and learning.[35]

Teachers, through their unified, widely-respected and encompassing union, the OAJ, are a very important part of the curriculum review process, reflecting Finland's strong tradition of co-operation between social partners.[36] The reviews are not affected by party-political agendas. Autonomy is then given to teachers and schools to implement the curriculum. This contrasts with a less agreed basis and structure for curriculum development, and regular party political gyrations over curriculum content, in Australia. The Abbott Government, for instance, soon after its election in 2013, imposed a two-person review of the national curriculum. Yet the national curriculum had been developed by the former national and all state and territory governments over the preceding six years, following some 20,000 submissions, and was yet to even be implemented. The Abbott Government's review appears to be motivated by a desire to see the curriculum focus less on the harsh treatment of indigenous people during and since Australia's colonisation and more on the claimed valiant struggle made since 1770 to bring the great British heritage into the Antipodes. Frank Sal believes that the ten-year review cycle in Finland gives teachers and schools a positive autonomy to implement and add to the curriculum without interference or

---

35   Halinen, 'Curriculum Reform in Finland'. The above also draws on valuable discussions I had with Petra Packalen, Counsellor of Education at the Finnish National Board of Education in Helsinki.

36   This point is emphasised by Jukka Sarjala in his article 'Equality and Co-operation: Finland's Path to Excellence', *American Educator*, Vol. 37, No. 1, Spring, 2013, pp. 32–36.

CHAPTER 3

interruptions from policy changes. 'All political parties support the country's education system and the processes' of curriculum review there, he emphasises.[37]

A recent historical study of Finland found that 75 per cent of Finnish people view the formation of the free, compulsory comprehensive school as the most important event in the nation's history. They rate it as more important than their crucial Winter War of 1939–1940 against the Soviet Union, more important than the winning of universal suffrage, more important than the welfare state, and more important than Finland's Civil War of 1918.[38] That the creation of the nine-year public institution which provides basic education to all, in the local areas in which they live, is viewed in such an exalted way is a striking indication of how deeply the Finns appreciate and value learning.

* * *

In Australia, the Labor Government elected in 2007 moved to introduce a more social democratic – as distinct from neo-liberal – element into education policy when the then Minister for Education, Julia Gillard, initiated in April 2010 a process for a fundamental review of school funding. This led to a new policy direction, influenced in part by evidence from Finland.

The diverse panel which was established to conduct this review, chaired by businessperson David Gonski, ensured multi-partisan

---

37   Milburn, 'With an Eye on the Finnish Line'.
38   Pilvi Torsti, *Suomalaiset ja Historia*, Gaudeamus Helsinki University Press, Helsinki, 2012, pp. 99–101 (as identified and translated by Ilkka Turunen, Special Government Adviser, Ministry of Education and Culture, Helsinki, Finland, in an interview which I conducted with him).

input and the taking of a long-term policy perspective. Thus the Gonski review was similar to Nordic-style commissions, which reflect the multi-party coalitions which usually make up governments in the Nordic nations due to their electoral systems of proportional representation. Such multi-partisan reviews and decision-making bodies, which necessarily seek to find common ground, are unusual in the more black-and-white, adversarial, short-term approaches which characterise Australian politics as a result of its mostly majoritarian electoral system.

The Gonski report was released in December 2011. Its general findings were that there is, in Australia, 'an unacceptable link between low levels of achievement and educational disadvantage, particularly among students from low socio-economic and Indigenous backgrounds'. It concluded that Australia must give its greatest 'support for its lowest performing students' and that to do this it needs new 'funding arrangements...where outcomes are not determined by socio-economic status or the type of school the child attends'. Instead, 'Australia needs effective arrangements for funding schools...that ensure resources are being provided where they are needed'.

'A significant increase in funding is required...with the largest part of this increase flowing to the government sector due to the significant numbers and greater concentration of disadvantaged students attending government schools'.[39]

The Gonski report identified how Finland significantly outperformed Australia in reading in PISA in both 2000 and 2009 and in Mathematics and Science in 2009. Australia's performance

---

39   David Gonski, Ken Boston, Kathryn Greiner, Carmen Lawrence, Bill Scales and Peter Tannock, *Review of Funding for Schooling – Final Report*, Australian Government, Canberra, December 2011, pp. xiii, xxiv, xv.

slippage in PISA was pronounced in mathematical literacy, with a decline from 47 to 38 per cent of students performing at Level 4 and above between 2000 and 2009, and an increase from 10 to 16 per cent of students performing below Level 2. In the 2009 PISA assessment of mathematical literacy, 17 per cent of Australian students achieved Level 5 or above compared to 22 per cent in Finland. 16 per cent of Australian students achieved below Level 2 compared to 8 per cent in Finland. The Gonski report noted evidence that the extent of inequality in a country, combined with particular characteristics of a country's schooling system, affect the possibilities for high educational outcomes. It identified quality teaching as undoubtedly being one of the most important in-school factors. It noted how Finland had sought to continually improve its schooling system through innovative approaches to learning. These approaches included adapting family support services and creating new kinds of schools. Finland, according to the Gonski report, demonstrates that it is possible to maintain a strongly high-performing *and* a consistently high-equity schooling system. Finland also demonstrates that it is possible to do a great deal to reduce the impact of a student's background on educational outcomes by investing in building the capacity of school leaders and teachers.[40]

The Australian Government's response to the Gonski report was issued in September 2012. Ms Gillard, now as Prime Minister, committed to move to a new funding system based on its recommendations, to take effect from 2014, with the transition to be completed by 2020. During 2013 the minority national Labor Government in Canberra sought to convince the states to accept its

---

40   Ibid. pp. 20, 109, 22, 23, 107, 110, 139.

plans for a 14.5 billion dollar increase in spending on schools to occur over the six years from 2014. Several state governments were reluctant to agree to the plan because it required them to put in large sums of money from their own budgets. Agreements for six-year funding were nevertheless reached before the September 2013 national election with four of the six states (New South Wales, Victoria, South Australia and Tasmania) and one of the two territories (the Australian Capital Territory). The other two states (Queensland and Western Australia) and the Northern Territory did not sign up.

However, the Right-of-centre Abbott Government, which defeated Labor in the September 2013 national election, continued the Liberal Party of Australia's long-term reluctance to support any move to more egalitarian public schooling. There was a major controversy in late November 2013 when its Education Minister Christopher Pyne indicated that he would abandon the entire Gonski plan, contrary to pre-election commitments to not do so. The Abbott government retreated from that position under enormous public pressure. However, it still only agreed to provide less than one-third of the money required under the agreements which had been reached with the four states and territory, by only committing to funding until the middle of 2017, i.e. for only four years instead of six. This decision was confirmed in the Abbott Government's first national budget, in May 2014. Yet the funding envisaged by Gonski and the former government for the fifth and sixth years is the most important, as it is that phase which is planned to deliver the largest new dollar amounts for disadvantaged schools. David Gonski has since cogently argued that the Abbott government can still, and should, reinstate the fifth and sixth years of funding which his report recommends. In doing so, he has reiterated what 'an eye opener' the experience of leading a major review of schools funding was for him as 'a businessman' in seeing just how 'enormous' is 'the difference between well-endowed schools and those in lower socio-economic areas' in Australia.[41]

Pasi Sahlberg, in direct contributions to debate about schools in Australia during September 2012, highlighted how competition between private and government schools is central in Australia. Such competition means that different school sectors and individual schools try to outdo each other according to the logic of a marketplace. Schools, principals and teachers increasingly compete for resources, for students, for staff and for parents. Sahlberg argued that this is not healthy, and nor does it achieve good results, compared with the different, collaborative approach which Finland has taken.[42] In Finland, he writes, there is, instead, 'mutual striving' for better schools.[43] He also emphasised during that Australian visit the need to enhance equity by managing choice in schooling. 'We have to decide whether we want to have choice for parents *or* equity. It is preferable that...there is choice within an equitable framework'.[44] In Finland, there is choice, but it is within each school and then, after year nine, it is between schools but not according to purchasing power. Rather the choice is between the content of the different specialisations which the various schools offer and how well these match individual students' particular interests and talents.

An important element of Finland's innovation and creativity is its readiness to allow students to take risks when learning, to think and

41 David Gonski, 'Jean Blackburn Oration', delivered at the University of Melbourne, 21 May 2014, pp. 3, 4.
42 Pasi Sahlberg, the University of Melbourne Graduate School of Education Dean's Lecture, 25 September 2012.
43 Sahlberg, *Finnish Lessons*, p. 36.
44 Pasi Sahlberg's comments at Australian National University Centre for European Studies workshop, Canberra, 27 September 2012.

try new things and, if some of these initially fail, then to learn from that experience for the future. This contrasts with a high pressure 'rote-learning' approach involving the instilling of 'facts', enforcing compliance with accepted knowledge, rewarding recitation of 'the right answer', which fails to foster innovation and creativity.

While in Australia in September 2012, Sahlberg, then the director of the Centre for International Mobility (CIMO) inside Finland's Ministry of Education and Culture, explicitly questioned the Gillard Government's aim for Australia to become one of the 'top five' schooling systems in the world by 2025. He pointed out that none of the current high-performing education systems in the OECD had achieved their place using the kind of policies Australia has pursued.[45] Besides Finland, the other four of the top five schooling systems based on the PISA 2009 reading scores were Shanghai, Hong Kong, Singapore and South Korea. It is noticeable that two of those four are not nations but rather are cities within China, which is explicitly not a democracy, and that the other two are not robust or renowned democracies. Schools in China are not going to encourage curiosity among young people to the extent of allowing questioning about what happened, for instance, in Tiananmen Square in 1989; nor will they encourage exploration of the principles of free speech. As such, it is puzzling, if we really believe in democracy, why they should be regarded as examples from which schools in democratic nations would want to learn or try to match.

Further, all four of the above countries – in sharp contrast to Finland – are associated with a learning approach that involves very long hours of authoritarian instruction and after-school, weekend

---

45   *The Age*, Melbourne, and *The Sydney Morning Herald*, 29 September 2012.

and 'holiday' work, in contrast to the more encouraging, curiosity-driven approach which Finland has taken so successfully. Sahlberg emphasises the considerable emphasis on wellbeing and play, and little homework in the early years of schooling, in the Finnish system.[46] He writes, on the basis of OECD statistics, that Finnish 15-year-old students spend less time on homework than do any of their peers in other nations, and that Finland's successes have come 'without private tutoring, after-school classes, or large amounts of homework, unlike...other countries'.[47] If Australia wants to achieve excellence in a way that brings alive the joy of learning in students, then Finland's approach is far more appropriate to pursue.

Pasi Sahlberg has also emphasised that Finland never set out to be a world leader in education.[48] It became a leader in educational quality after it set a goal to ensure a good school for every child in the nation. That, therefore, will be a more appropriate goal for Australia to now set – or to now reaffirm, in the spirit of the Gonski panel recommendations.

Another reason for its positive educational outcomes is that Finland takes a broader and more inclusive approach to defining 'special needs' students than elsewhere. Finland also makes more assistance programs available to meet students' special needs. There is close attention to meeting every student's needs as an individual. These features were noted by Frank Sal during the 2012 study tour of Finland in which he participated. Sal observed that 'Finland's student assessment system is backed by a strong, ongoing intervention program for all students found to be struggling either

---

46   Pasi Sahlberg's lecture at the University of Melbourne, 25 September 2012.
47   Sahlberg, *Finnish Lessons*, pp. 62, 37.
48   Ibid. p. 41.

academically or behaviourally. All schools have teams of special education teachers who usually work in pairs with a maximum of twelve students in a group'. In Finland, he reported, 'seven per cent of their education budget goes into special needs support, compared with one per cent of our education budget' and 50 per cent of all Finnish students are helped by special needs teachers at some stage of their schooling.[49] The proportion of Australian students assisted is miniscule by comparison. As Pasi Sahlberg explains, in Finland the high participation and comprehensive coverage means that 'special education is nothing special anymore'. The Finnish approach 'significantly reduces the negative stigma that is often brought on by special education' in other contexts.[50] Ari Pokka adds that 'special education teachers not only help the students but actually help very much the other teachers'.[51]

Frank Sal is passionate about:

> one of the greatest strengths of the Finnish system being that, through the additional care given to students, they identify needs at a very early stage. Students who are identified as falling behind in any way are immediately supported by additional staff. Students who are right at the top, who teachers feel might not be being extended adequately, receive support as well. So the entire school 'special assistance' support is much greater than we have any capacity for here in Australia, because we just do not have the resources for it.[52]

Sal noticed that Finnish schools also have 'a nurse who works with students and their families on health problems. National principal[s']

---

49   Milburn, 'With an Eye on the Finnish Line'.
50   Sahlberg, *Finnish Lessons*, p. 47.
51   Pokka interview.
52   Interview with Frank Sal.

CHAPTER 3

organisations in Australia have been campaigning for a similar approach to early intervention and welfare services in their schools'.[53] He and his colleagues on the Finnish study tour were impressed by how 'a strong student welfare system provides intervention...[for] all students in need...[including with] student counsellors'.[54] There is in Finland a strong focus on student welfare, health and wellbeing at no charge to students. This includes, at Cygnaeus Upper Secondary School for example, the *kuraattori* or social worker meeting once a week with a group of students who may be having motivational or other difficulties, with a focus on helping them to develop practical solutions.[55] The effectiveness of this broad special needs approach has helped to lessen the harsh policy of grade repetition (that is, repeating an entire year of schooling for not having passed some particular subjects). The incidence of grade repetition in Australia in 2012 was double that of Finland's, which, in addition to its disproportionate severity, adds considerably to costs.[56]

Visiting Australian school principals noted the 'hot healthy lunches to promote physical wellbeing'[57] which are provided free daily in all Finnish schools. Separately visiting Australian teacher unionist Susan Hopgood also noticed these and emphasised how:

> it's not just any old lunch, they don't just throw them a sandwich, they have choices, they line up at the cafeteria, it's hot, there's salads. The kids...[then]...sit at tables. It's not only about making

53 Milburn, 'With an Eye on the Finnish Line'.
54 Australian School Principals' Report of their 2012 study tour of Finland.
55 Pokka interview.
56 Andreas Schleicher, *Equity, Excellence and Inclusiveness in Education: Policy Lessons from around the World*, OECD, Paris, 2014, pp. 80, 78.
57 Australian School Principals' Report of their 2012 study tour of Finland.

sure that the children are well fed, it's also about...social skills... school has a role to play here.

> It struck me that [when]...the principal came and had lunch with us...the kids were very much at ease about coming up and talking to the principal...talking to the teachers and all the interactions.[58]

Ari Pokka, in discussions with me, likewise pointed to the relative informality of Finnish schools. Such arrangements may enhance greater genuine respect by students towards teachers than formal, traditional arrangements. Part of this informality is that school uniforms have never been worn in Finland. Many people in Australia, as in Britain, support school uniforms as part of the egalitarian purpose of school education, as they can prevent poorer children and young people from appearing less well-presented than those who can afford more expensive clothes. However, the old stock-standard, often grey or navy blue uniforms have, over several decades, been outdone by some schools adopting elaborate, brightly coloured, embroidered blazers and the like. With their gold monogrammed crests, insignia, ornamental trim and brocade, these deliberately mark out the students of the elite, privileged, mostly private, fee-charging schools as of higher status than those wearing more basic school uniforms from less well-off schools.

Pasi Sahlberg is very positive about the move by Alberta, Canada, to reduce control of school testing, and to move away from standardised competitive tests in favour of more intelligent accountability policies that focus on authentic learning. This, he argues, has led Alberta to become more educationally successful than all other

---

58   Hopgood interview.

provinces in Canada. He identifies how particular states of Australia have similar population sizes to Finland and may be in a position to likewise adapt Finnish approaches.[59] The fact that Canada is more multicultural than Finland has not prevented Alberta from successfully taking these steps.

Frank Sal has indicated that there is interest from his Finnish counterparts in the way Australian schools meet the needs of students from diverse cultural backgrounds. Pasi Sahlberg makes the important point that Finland's level of student performance continuously increased, and variation in student performance decreased, *while* Finnish society became more culturally diverse. In other words, Finland successfully increased excellence and equity at the same time as it increased ethnic and cultural diversity.[60] There has also long been a formal constitutional requirement in Finland that the Sami people are entitled to attend schools conducted in their own languages. No such provision has existed in Australia. If it had, indigenous languages could have been better preserved. Finland's constitution also requires that members of the nation's Swedish-speaking minority are entitled to attend schools conducted in their own language. Official Finnish documents emphasise how 'the same opportunities to education should be available to all citizens irrespective of their ethnic origin, age, wealth or where they live'.[61]

The following comments made by the Australian school principals following their study tour of Finland express well the characteristics

59 Sahlberg, *Finnish Lessons*, pp. 67–68, 98, 8.
60 Ibid. p. 69.
61 Ministry of Education and Culture, Finnish National Board of Education and CIMO, *Finnish Education in a Nutshell*, Kopijyvä, Espoo, 2012, pp. 5, 7.

of Finnish education which its funding arrangements help to make possible and from which other nations can draw inspiration:

> the belief in making a difference for each and every child... ensures a supportive learning environment where every child is nurtured at their level of development to reach their potential.

> ...The nature of intervention involves a structured progression through a well-planned and defined curriculum...ensuring that when support is provided the child continues his/her journey of learning in a manner which is not disruptive and which deliberately builds and consolidates the learning progression without damaging self-esteem and the learner's self-belief in their ability.[62]

The logical companion of Finland's deep appreciation of education has been its heavy investment in research and development to become a knowledge economy. This investment has seen Finland recover strongly from the global economic setbacks of the early 1990s and of 2008–2009.

The exiting now of its iconic Nokia brand from mobile phone production, after an illustrious and pioneering global prominence in that sphere over two decades, does not invalidate the success which Finland achieved with Nokia and mobile phones, nor the principles by which it did so. The biggest benefits from the latest mobile phone to become financially dominant in the world – the iPhone – continue to be received by nations with highly skilled workforces which are capable of undertaking the complex tasks in its manufacture. Those workers are capable of doing this, in turn, because their governments have invested more heavily in research and development than other countries, in order to become knowledge economies; just as Finland

---

62 Australian School Principals' Report of their 2012 study tour of Finland.

did with Nokia.[63] A 'Nokia bridge' program and other measures have been provided to help the people who worked at the corporation – many of whom were graduates of Finland's high quality vocational education – to cope with the new circumstances. These have limited the negative employment consequences of Nokia's transition by enabling very many former Nokia workers to take their information and communications technology skills into Finland's public sector, or into other sectors, or to set up new businesses utilising their experience which will help Finland to reposition for future opportunities. The positive role which employment adjustment programs such as this play for adult workers in Nordic nations, in particular as they apply in Denmark, is the focus of the next chapter.

---

63   More than one-third of the money paid for each Apple iPhone goes to Japan because that is where some of its most advanced components are made, whereas 17 per cent goes to Germany, whose precision manufacturers pay wages higher than those paid to American manufacturing workers. Of the money paid for each iPhone – although the product is assembled in China and owned by the American Apple corporation – only 3.6 per cent goes to China and only 6 per cent goes to the USA. See the post made on 18 July 2012 at http://robertreich.org.

SKILLING UP SECURELY: DENMARK'S INVESTMENT IN TRAINING AND PROVISION OF SECURITY, AS WELL AS FLEXIBILITY, IN PEOPLE'S EMPLOYMENT LIVES

A central question for this chapter is what Australia can learn from Denmark about providing substantial skills retraining opportunities for the mature-age unemployed now and in the future. Their numbers will rise further in Australia following an estimated fall in national employment of as many as 200,000 people because of the planned closure of all three Australian car makers by 2017.[1] This will be in addition to the loss of that industry's considerable research and development activity.

There has been a dramatic decline of employment in many steel and manufacturing centres in Australia since the 1970s, including in

---

1   Bianca Barbaro, John Spoehr and the National Institute for Economic and Industry Research (NIEIR), *Closing the Motor Vehicle Industry: The Impact on Australia*, Australian Workplace Innovation and Social Research Centre, Adelaide and NIEIR, The University of Adelaide, 2014, p. 3.

many suburbs within some capital cities. One of the lessons which has been learned from these experiences is that you cannot just take middle-aged workers out of factory environments, put them into classrooms and then expect them to immediately learn new skills for new jobs in that unfamiliar setting.

Denmark has had to grapple with a similar decline of heavy industry, including shipbuilding, over recent decades. As this chapter will later outline, some Australians during the last decade have sought to bring home lessons from Denmark's comparative success in adapting to these trends. Yet their observations and recommendations have gone largely unheeded. Unless Australia does now start to learn from Danish experience, Australia's economic and social problems are going to seriously worsen.

* * *

Professor Andrew Beer has studied one of the areas in Australia affected by employment decline: the southern suburbs of Adelaide in the first decade of the 21st century after it was hit by the closure of Mitsubishi car-making operations. He found that, of those workers made redundant, one-third never worked again. 'A third of the workers moved into full time paid employment, a third of the workers moved into what we think of as casual or contract employment, and a third of the workers left the workforce entirely,' he says. Beer outlines how the shutdown of Mitsubishi's Lonsdale foundry in 2004 and then its Tonsley Park engine-making plant in 2008 had a devastating impact on the lives of many workers. Adelaide's southern suburbs suffered an economic shock, which is still being felt. Beer says that it is important for decision-makers to keep such effects in mind when considering car workers' futures around Australia now. Of the workers made redundant from the closures, those who had formal qualifications were far more likely to find employment after one or two years than those who had very few qualifications. 'Often you hear relatively dry economics arguments around "well this is just a process of structural adjustment", but in fact these are real people having their lives affected in a very real way,' he says. With these words, Beer makes a very important point which needs to be registered by those who smooth over aggregate employment statistics to minimise and downplay the deep human consequences of pain and hardship felt by the many who go prematurely from paid work into the ranks of the often hidden unemployed. 'Effectively you saw a loss of skills over the South Australian workforce', as well as 'diminished earnings for those affected individuals', Beer goes on to say. He warns that the imminent exit of all car makers from Australia will be felt for generations. He urges governments to move quickly to ensure that workers are given the opportunity to learn new skills before the plants close.[2] He adds that these upcoming closures will be worse in their impact than previous shutdowns because of the fact that three major car manufacturers will be closing across Australia at a similar time.[3]

Another analyst of adaptations to past downturns in the South Australian economy, since the international economic recession of the 1990s, is Rodin Genoff. He has worked as a practitioner in economic adjustment initiatives in another hard-hit former car-making region in that state: Elizabeth, north of Adelaide. Genoff has since gone on to carry out regional development analyses and projects in central

2   Professor Beer is from the University of Adelaide. His comments were made on
      Australian Broadcasting Corporation (hereafter ABC) news online, 11 December
      2013.
3   *The Age*, Melbourne, 15 February 2014.

and northern Denmark, following interest taken in his work by the OECD. I asked him to compare his experiences in Australia with those in Denmark, and specifically whether the Danish context of 'Flexicurity', and the substantially higher public investment in skills retraining opportunities there, makes a positive difference to the prospects of mature-aged unemployed workers in Denmark, compared with Australia. He replied that these make a 'massive difference', particularly for workers in (former) manufacturing regions.[4] 'Flexicurity' is especially important in managing downturns in the business cycle and the pressures for adjustment which arise from companies' increased exposure to the global economy, he adds. He further contends that there is 'absolutely less' regional inequality in Denmark than Australia. This may be partly because Denmark is a smaller nation, but evidence does show that 'Denmark displays the lowest income disparities across regions' of *all* OECD economies.[5]

Also of interest is a study of how much the comprehensive Danish welfare state helped workers and their families to adjust to the closure during the 1980s of a major shipyard in Nakskov, a town which had grown up around the shipbuilding industry. The authors of that study found that, in part through 'large-scale net income transfers between Danish regions', the 'Danish welfare state…operates as a major element in regional economic equalisation policy' and 'plays an important role in preventing regional and local economic inequality in Denmark from reaching serious proportions'. During the closure of the Nakskov shipyard, the Danish welfare state reacted 'in a compensatory and regionally differentiated manner', to the benefit of Nakskov and

4   Interview with Rodin Genoff.
5   OECD, *OECD Reviews of Regional Innovation: Central and Southern Denmark 2012*, OECD, Paris, p. 16.

other poor areas. This was then supplemented by European Union community support and social funds to help transform the Nakskov area as a region affected by the decline of a particular industry. The funds were used to support productive investment, especially in food, electronics and new metal products industries; to provide vocational training and enhanced management skills; and to improve the local physical environment and infrastructure.[6] Although the job losses amounted to 2,500 out of Nakskov's population of 30,000 people, a very high proportion of the displaced workers were able to move into new jobs in the metal and other industries. Partly this was because there were active programs to provide support *before* the workers left their old jobs, as a result of the local employment service working constructively and early with the company and using a combination of public and company funds for this purpose.[7]

According to Genoff, 'Flexicurity' also helps Danish workers to develop the range of multiple skills which they need to manage today's intelligent machinery, including crossing the traditional divide between metal work and electronics, and also to gain the depth of skills expertise needed for those respective trades.

The word 'Flexicurity' is an awkward and not very attractive way of trying to bring together the two often opposed concepts of 'flexibility' and 'security'. It was first used not by a Dane, but rather by a Dutch minister of Social Affairs and Employment in 1995 to describe a law aimed at giving more job security for temporary workers and less

6   Frank Hansen and Chris Jensen-Butler, 'Economic Crisis and the Regional and Local Economic Effects of the Welfare State: The Case of Denmark', *Regional Studies*, Vol. 30, No. 2, 1996, pp. 176, 184, 177, 180, 183.

7   Interview with Jan Hendeliowitz, currently chief policy adviser in the Danish Agency for Labour Market and Recruitment (formerly the National Labour Market Authority) who, at the time of the Nakskov shipyard closure, was the director of the local employment service which assisted the displaced workers.

for 'permanent' workers: i.e. to spread employment security arrangements more evenly across the labour force of the Netherlands.[8] There was considerable European interest in the notion of 'Flexicurity' in the mid-2000s. That interest has since dissipated, however, as many proponents of 'Flexicurity' in parts of Europe kept focusing on the flexibility for employers to dismiss workers, and not mentioning its two other crucial components as it operates in Denmark. Denmark's trade union confederation, the Danish *Landsorganisationen* or LO, issued a publication in 2008 making it crystal clear that it is a basis of economic security which crucially underpins Danish workers' flexibility between particular jobs.[9] Denmark's three-pronged approach to employment policy does involve flexible rules for hiring and firing: but also, and crucially, it involves the provision of generous unemployment benefits for those who have lost jobs; *and* further, and just as crucially, it involves the provision of substantial and effective Active Labour Market Programs (ALMPs), and quality training, to help unemployed people gain new skills for new jobs. This Danish approach came to be closely identified with the term 'Flexicurity', especially after the OECD held Denmark up as a shining example in 2004. In reality though, this three-pronged employment policy is a very long-standing approach reached as a result of contests and compromises between unions and employers. It has evolved in Denmark over more than a century. The balance did, however, change somewhat in Denmark from the mid-1990s when the Social Democrats then in government considerably boosted spending on the ALMPs component. This increase in investment formed the basis for

8   Interview with Professor Per Kongshøj Madsen.
9   Harald Børsting, *A Flexible Labour Market Needs Strong Social Partners: The European Discussion on the Danish Labour Market*, LO, Copenhagen, 2008.

the association of the Danish three-pronged employment approach with the term 'Flexicurity'.

The Australian Council of Social Service (ACOSS) has highlighted that Australia has the lowest level of unemployment benefits in the OECD for a single person recently unemployed. Denmark has one of the highest levels. ACOSS compares the social security and housing payments made to people in their first year of unemployment in different countries, expressed as a proportion of a low full-time wage. The proportions are: 40 per cent for a single person with no children in Australia, compared with 84 per cent in Denmark; 53 per cent for a person in a double-income household with no children in Australia compared with 91 per cent in Denmark; 60 per cent for a sole parent with two children in Australia compared with 90 per cent in Denmark; and 69 per cent for a person in a double-income household in Australia with two children, compared with 93 per cent in Denmark.[10]

Australia's employment services system, meanwhile, tends to reward private businesses which give priority to the most easily placed of the unemployed. It does not give enough resources to providers who can offer the most disadvantaged jobseekers the intensive, individually tailored services and help which they need.[11] Case management often does not start until long into unemployment, and it is not as comprehensive as it was in association with the short-lived suite of ALMPs which was introduced by the Labor Government in Australia in the early to mid-1990s. Denmark, like Sweden (as was discussed in Chapter 2 on page 88), has much stronger and

---

10   ACOSS, *Surviving, Not Living*, Submission to Senate Employment Committee on the Adequacy of 'Allowance' Payments, ACOSS Paper 192, Sydney, August 2012, pp. 45–46.

11   ACOSS, *Towards More Efficient and Responsive Employment Services*, ACOSS Paper 184, Sydney, 2012, p. 5.

more supportive employment assistance and active labour market arrangements to assist the jobless.

There are 94 integrated job centres for all job seekers in Denmark. These operate at municipal level, which is intended in part to ensure that they are responsive to local labour market trends. The centres are responsible for direct contact with the unemployed, and for identifying each person's particular situation and existing skills. Their staff conduct interviews with the unemployed or prospective unemployed persons, provide counselling, actively help job seekers to compose an individual action plan and also help them to gain time and resources from their current employer to look for new jobs in advance. The scale of investment in reskilling programs in Denmark enables job centre caseworkers to be broad-minded about the possibilities for fundamental career change, which they can suggest to unemployed workers. They can, for instance, support, and have in some cases supported, the transition of male workers from the industry of shipbuilding, which has declined, into working in care for the elderly, which is growing.

A comparative study of employment services in the two nations has found that 'the Danish case managers operated quite differently to their Australian counterparts. They were, for example, more attuned and responsive to the social and environmental issues confronting their clients, and they displayed considerably more discretion and autonomy in the way they worked' to take into account 'social' factors 'in their understanding of unemployment'. By contrast 'Australian case managers...were significantly more constrained, and operated in a manner congruent with the punitive policy context that they work within. They were also less able to use discretion to mitigate the effects of these policies because they themselves were subject to a range of organisational performance measures that focused on achieving certain output targets'.[12]

A Danish Government Expert Committee on active labour market policy which reported in 2014 also recommends – in contrast to the ever more punitive direction of policy in Australia – the introduction into Denmark of certain *rights* to education and training for the unemployed who do not have formal competencies, as they are most at risk of long-term unemployment. These include the right to an assessment of real (non-formal) competencies, the right to basic courses in reading, writing and mathematics, as well as the right to vocational education for unemployed persons most in need, who it identifies as being lower-skilled unemployed people aged 30 or over. The Committee further recommends that all unemployed persons obtain the right to six weeks of job-targeted training after six months of unemployment. The Committee, in addition, declares the following as rights: the right to short, job-oriented courses with a job guarantee for the long-term unemployed; and the right to specifically tailored courses for unemployed people who suffer from dyslexia.

Significantly, and also in clear contrast with the direction of Australian policy, the Danish Expert Committee recommends the abolition of procedural requirements on the unemployed regarding interviews, and the abolition of obligations to participate in repeated active measures. It makes this recommendation in order to achieve 'a greater focus on contents and results'. If that proposal is adopted, then unemployed persons in Denmark will only be obliged to participate in one activating course after six months of unemployment, and this

---

12   Greg Marston, Jørgen Elm Larsen and Catherine McDonald, 'The Active Subjects of Welfare Reform: A Street-Level Comparison of Employment Services in Australia and Denmark', *Social Work and Society*, Vol. 3, No. 2, 2005, p. 154.

course will always be connected to an enterprise, as such measures prove most effective.[13]

The most persistent advocate in Australia of the Danish approach to upskilling workers to prevent and adapt to job losses has been Tim Colebatch, the former and long-time economics editor of *The Age* newspaper in Melbourne. Colebatch wrote, for example, in 2005, about how 'Australia could learn something about training from the Danes'. He argued that:

> at a time when skills shortages have slowed Australia's growth, we should look hard at the country that leads the world in job training. Since the mid-1990s, Denmark has tackled skills short-ages and unemployment by its own ambitious version of mutual obligation. It requires unemployed people to undergo educat-ion and training to equip them with the skills the economy needs, and which they need to find work. In Australia, mutual obligation has done nothing to meet the country's skills short-age because we are doing it on the cheap, sending people off to work-for-the-dole projects that do little or nothing for their job prospects. Denmark has done it seriously, and it works.[14]

In Australia, the term 'mutual obligation' was introduced by the Howard Government to replace the former Labor Government's term 'reciprocal obligation'. There was much quibbling about the semantic differences between these two terms. However, there was a difference of substance. The *Working Nation* ALMPs which were eventually introduced under the Keating Government following Australia's descent into the international recession of the early 1990s

---

13   Summary (in English) of the recommendations of the Committee's report titled *Veje til Job – En Arbejdsmarkedsindsats med Mening: Ekspertgruppen om Udredning af den Aktive Beskæftigelsesindsats*, Danish Ministry of Employment, Copenhagen, February 2014, p. 8.

14   *The Age*, Melbourne, 15 March 2005.

– but which were then abolished by the Howard Government – envisaged the government's obligation as extending to providing skills training for the unemployed. The programs were based on a premise that a government's obligation to unemployed people is more than just the payment of a bare subsistence unemployment benefit.

Colebatch, in his March 2005 article, was criticising the lack of skills training in the Howard Government's so-called 'mutual obligation'. Colebatch emphatically endorsed the OECD's findings that 'individuals who participate in training have a higher probability of being employed', that 'adult learning has a durable impact on individual employment prospects' and that 'wages grow faster after training'.[15] He also wrote in that article about how Danish labour economist Flemming Larsen told an Australian conference the previous month that by boosting and keeping such programs going during the 1990s in Denmark, 'unemployment was halved in five years, causing hardly any bottlenecks or inflationary problems. The problems with structural unemployment and the negative con-sequences of passive (unemployment) schemes [thus] seem[ed] to have been solved'.

The unemployment rate in Denmark, with its high investment in ALMPS, was lower in all but one of the 14 years of economic upswing from the early 1990s recession, until the effects of the GFC were felt in 2009, than was the unemployment rate in Australia, with its non-investment in ALMPs.[16] The Danish policy approach was clearly superior at channelling economic growth into jobs growth.

---

15   Ibid., quoting OECD, *OECD Employment Outlook 2004*, OECD, Paris, 2004, pp. 192, 198.

16   *OECD Historical Statistics 1970–2000*, Table 2.14 and *OECD Employment Outlook 2013*, Statistical Annex, Table A.

CHAPTER 4

Flemming Larsen's paper formed part of the ongoing work of the Danish National Centre for Labour Market Research (CARMA) at Aalborg University in Denmark. One of Larsen's colleagues from that Centre, who also participated in the 2005 Australian conference, is Professor Per Kongshøj Madsen. These analysts bring a welcome, broadening social policy dimension into the analysis of employment programs. Orthodox labour market economists often tend to be too narrow and technical in their measurements.

Denmark does nevertheless rigorously review its programs to ensure that they are being effective. For example, 17 out of 19 Danish and international studies have found positive effects from its private wage-subsidy programs.[17]

Tim Colebatch has continued to write regularly about what a small fraction Australia spends on training the unemployed compared to Denmark.[18] Recent available data on this point indicates that *Denmark spends nearly eight times the public funds that Australia does on ALMPs.*[19] Colebatch has identified how Denmark's approach means that retrenched workers do not receive redundancy payments but that they instead receive immediate retraining. (A similar observation was made by Laurie Carmichael about Sweden's arrangements in the 1980s: see page 49.) The retraining is supported with public funds, often in the form of wage subsidies, as well as the intensive publicly funded help which is given for the workers to find new jobs. These active measures mean that Denmark has one of the Western world's

---

17 Material in Danish provided and translated by Jan Hendeliowitz and sourced from http://ams.dk/da/Arbejdsmarkedsstyrelsen.aspx and http://www.jobindsats.dk/.

18 e.g. Tim Colebatch, 'Australia Lagging on Helping Unemployed Back to Work', *The Age*, Melbourne, 12 July 2010, which refers to OECD, *OECD Employment Outlook 2010*, OECD, Paris, 2010, Statistical Annex, Table K.

19 *OECD Employment Outlook 2013*, Statistical Annex, Table P.

highest rates of 'older' people who are still in paid work. Labour force participation rates in Denmark in general – and for 'prime-age' persons, i.e. those aged 25 to 54 – have long been very much higher than the rates in Australia.[20]

Colebatch has acknowledged that a move to Danish-style spending on ALMPs will initially 'cost money', but he argues that 'it will do Australia far more good than big tax cuts' as 'we cannot go on underinvesting in people without serious and lasting social and economic consequences'.[21]

One of the organisers of the Australian conference mentioned by Colebatch in his March 2005 *Age* article was former Labor social security minister and deputy prime minister Brian Howe. Colebatch wrote then how Brian Howe 'focused that conference partly on Denmark, seeing it as a model from which to learn'. This was because of the way that Denmark sees 'a key role for government is to manage "transitional labour markets" to minimise the risks facing displaced workers and "make transitions pay" by lifetime learning' to increase those workers' continuing employment prospects. Brian Howe elaborated these ideas in a book in 2007. In this, he emphasised that people's lives are characterised by major transitions. As well as the major change which many people make at particular points in their lives to become parents, the transitions include: from formal education to employment; often at some point from employed to unemployed; from health to some form and degree of incapacity; and from full-time paid work to reduced paid work and then retirement. Howe argues that governments can help people to manage those transitions

---

20 *OECD Historical Statistics*, Table 2.2 and annual issues of *OECD Employment Outlook*, Statistical Annex, Table C.

21 Tim Colebatch, 'We've Failed the Jobless', *The Age*, Melbourne, 18 April 2006.

better by substantially investing in lifelong learning. Howe expressed concern that, in Australia, 'workers with less skill are much less likely to participate in training than are higher skilled workers' and that 'higher skilled employees are more likely to have employers pay for their training than less skilled employees are'. He therefore advocated 'lifelong learning accounts': an approach similar to superannuation, with funds being built up to finance further education and training throughout people's working lives. 'Matching contributions of one per cent of salary would be contributed by employers and employees, with a one per cent government contribution for low-wage workers,' Howe proposed.[22]

These ideas have since been taken further, towards specific practical proposals for policy change in Australia, by Grant Belchamber, at the time the economist for the ACTU, and now its international officer, in papers which followed interviews and information he gathered during a study tour of Denmark in 2009. Belchamber argues that 'by adopting a social insurance model, Australia can raise significantly the income support available to unemployed workers'. He describes how, in Denmark, 'unions stress that "Flexicurity" means flexibility *for* workers, not of workers'. Further, in the Danish context, 'flexibility does not mean wage concessions'. Rather, 'it is a means by which life-cycle considerations and transitions' come into 'managing work-life balance'. 'Fairly and properly constructed provisions on working time flexibility are essential components of the...[policy] that operates in...Denmark.' The nation has a 'focus on life-long learning and skills acquisition through working life [which]

---

22   Brian Howe, *Weighing up Australian Values: Balancing Transitions and Risks to Work and Family in Modern Australia*, UNSW Press, Sydney, 2007, pp. 133, 134, 141, 142.

delivers a high-skill and high-competence workforce and society, with correspondingly high average earnings'.[23]

Belchamber identifies how in Denmark 'payments to unemployed workers come from two sources. "Social assistance" is similar to Australian unemployment benefits' in that 'payment is a low flat rate, is generally available, is means-tested and assets-tested, and continuation is conditional on recipients meeting activity tests and accepting activating measures'. However, in Denmark, 'in addition, all workers can opt in to unemployment insurance schemes' in which 'benefit payments rise according to earnings in the previous job'. Through that means, 'the minimum payment delivers a "replacement rate" [i.e. the proportion of the person's wage earnings in her/his previous job] of around 90 per cent for low paid workers...These benefits are delivered out of dedicated funds run by unions'. The proportion of the workforce covered by unemployment insurance funds in Denmark is approximately 75 per cent. As Belchamber writes, the 'funds are also used to provide top-up pay for employees on shortened hours who are engaged in workplace training...for example, in firms [which were] affected by the GFC. Workers who are in that situation 'receive wages for hours worked and...payments for time spent in training'.[24] The 27 unemployment insurance funds associated with trade unions in Denmark also play an active role in helping their members who have lost their jobs to plan to reskill for new work.

Belchamber describes how 'employers notify the unions concerned of their intention to lay off workers'. Unions then 'negotiate the number of redundancies', taking into account the 'employer's skill

---

23 Grant Belchamber, 'Flexicurity: What Is It? Can It Work Down Under?', *Australian Bulletin of Labour*, Vol. 36, No. 3, 2010, pp. 278, 282, 283 (my emphasis).
24 Ibid. pp. 283, 284.

requirements'. In Denmark, 'more than 95 per cent of the workforce will access unemployment insurance, social assistance or both at one or more points during their working lives. While there is a measure of *job* security in their labour markets, the emphasis in the Nordic countries is overtly and overwhelmingly on *employment* security'. Belchamber notes that 'the most common criticism levelled at "Flexicurity" is its cost. Market fundamentalists point to Denmark...[as] having [among] the highest ratios of taxation revenue to GDP in the world'. He acknowledges that 'Flexicurity' 'cannot be delivered on the cheap'. However, like Colebatch, he sees the medium- and long-term benefits from this expenditure – including the starkly higher rates of workforce participation and the huge social as well as economic benefits which these bring – as clearly being worth the short-term cost.[25]

According to Belchamber, 'countries with low unemployment benefit payments' such as Australia therefore now 'should raise them relative to wage incomes', thus increasing the extent to which those benefits replace previous wage earnings. Belchamber is confident that 'Flexicurity' 'can work anywhere if the suite of policies is sufficiently comprehensive and the society's commitment to them is strong'. He points out that Australia already has a flexible labour market, as evidenced by the fact that 'the median length of job duration is around three years, well below most OECD economies and broadly in line with Denmark'. Further, there are, in Australia, 'high levels of internal...flexibility too, with broad and encompassing job definitions and skill-based classifications'. Essentially, he argues, given that Australia already has a flexible labour market, but does not have

---

25   Ibid. pp. 285, 289 (my emphasis).

either substantial investment in ALMPs or adequate unemployment benefits, it could now benefit from the *addition* of those elements.[26]

Belchamber has since adapted his earlier papers into a book chapter in which he writes that, in Australia, 'the extremely low [benefit] replacement rate…[is] wholly inadequate…to keep families functionally intact during job transitions'. He also, more generally, praises 'the "Flexicurity" policy suite' pursued by Denmark as 'a rich policy response that [has] recognised the complexities inherent in combining economic growth with social inclusion, rejecting the simple policy prescriptions of Anglo-centric economic orthodoxy'. He emphasises how, in Denmark, of the 'workers who lose their jobs…depending on economic conditions, some/most…will quickly find alternative employment in decent work'. However, 'for some workers…including those working in industries and occupations affected by structural change' – and who are therefore similar to many of the car industry workers now facing retrenchment in Australia – 'there may be no job openings in the industries or occupations from which they have been displaced'.[27]

In Denmark, 'soon after losing their jobs, these workers have the capacity…and obligation…to undertake a program of (re)training, to upgrade their skills or acquire an entirely new skill set'. This is possible there because the adequate 'unemployment benefits available to them provide motivation and income support for the duration of the training program'. Further, for its part, the state has an obligation to provide an adequate range of quality skills training programs for the unemployed. 'Equipped with a new or renewed set of skills in

---

26   Ibid. pp. 289, 290, 291.
27   Grant Belchamber, 'To Fix a Flaw and Fix the Floor: Unemployment Insurance for Australia' in Paul Smyth and John Buchanan (eds.), *Inclusive Growth in Australia: Social Policy as Economic Investment*, Allen and Unwin, Sydney, 2013, pp. 193, 195, 196.

demand, and/or having participated in capacity-building work experience programs,' very large proportions of Danish 'unemployed workers re-enter employment in the flexible labour market'.[28]

Belchamber explains that 'the "Flexicurity" conception is of "transitions" through a multiplicity of alternative states. In a dynamic world – today and increasingly tomorrow – the vast majority of workers will have a succession of jobs with a series of different employers, intermingled with...further study/training' and possibly some periods of unemployment. 'Each successive transition shapes the next one; success breeds further success; and every failure increases the baggage to be carried into the subsequent transition. The challenge for policy [now] is to "make transitions pay"', he writes.[29]

However, he goes on to write:

> Australia['s] unemployment benefit is so abysmally low...[that it] is...insufficient for an unemployed person – whether a displaced worker or long-term jobless – to find a good new job, let alone undertake any career-renewing training or skills program of quality and substance. Further, the application of strict income and assets tests conditions [for] eligibility for receipt of... [unemployment] benefits...[means that] a prime-age worker displaced from their job by economic crisis or restructuring must first expend their cash savings, and in addition their partner's income must be extremely low.[30]

Belchamber concludes that 'there are two flaws in our labour market floor: funding for our labour market activation programs is meagre, and their effectiveness is questionable; and our unemployment benefit replacement rates are miserly'. In response, there needs to be 'training

---

28   Ibid. p. 196.
29   Ibid.
30   Ibid. pp. 199, 200.

programs...[to] help many jobless people to improve their skills so they can compete for jobs once the economy recovers'.[31]

He reflects on how:

> Australia's unemployment benefits system originated in an era when work was [always assumed to be] full-time and done by male breadwinners, and unemployment was transitory...Its good features are that it is publicly funded and universal. But in an era of rapid and continuous technological change, skills become obsolete at an unprecedented pace, and workers increasingly hold a...[large] number of different jobs over the course of their working life.[32]

Therefore, he argues, 'a new, comprehensive...unemployment insurance scheme in parallel with Australia's...industry super-annuation schemes has great long-term promise'. In the same way that 'superannuation is about income security during retirement... unemployment insurance is about income security during working life'. He envisages that 'there are many possible variants of a viable national scheme'. These include 'premium levels, benefit payments, activation requirements, degree of compulsion, eligibility criteria, the role of government and more'. He then reports in detail on how 'for the purposes of establishing quantitative "proof of concept" for un-employment insurance in Australia, the ACTU [has] investigated the level of benefit that would be available under an illustrative scheme in which a payment of one per cent of gross wages was made for unemployment income insurance cover in a nationally pooled scheme'. Based on various 'modelling specifications', this 'exploratory actuarial costing' indicates that 'the scheme is economically feasible

---

31   Ibid. p. 201.
32   Ibid. p. 202.

and sustainable'. Belchamber therefore proposes 'adoption of a social insurance model for payment of wage-related unemployment benefits in Australia'. Even though this 'would represent a major departure from national historical practice', it is warranted in his view because 'in conjunction with a better suite of activating labour market programs, it would fix a major flaw in Australia's social protection floor'.[33]

* * *

The Ministry of Education in Denmark emphasises a holistic approach to adult education, influenced by the ideas of the 19th century Danish educational thinker, N.F.S. Grundtvig, who believed that it is important to provide free opportunities to enable people to make discoveries and to undertake creative learning for life. Available internationally comparative statistics suggest that the rate of participation in job-related education by adults is 22 per cent in Australia compared with 35 per cent in Denmark.[34] In Denmark, there are more than one million participations a year in *ArbejdsMarkedsUddannelser* or *AMU*, meaning adult vocational training, by more than half a million Danes.[35] This suggests that more than one in every 14 of the adult Danish population is participating in vocational training programs.[36] Most of the participations involve a part-time-commitment, while 15,500 are full-time. These data

---

33   Ibid. pp. 202, 203, 204.

34   OECD, *Education at a Glance 2011*, OECD, Paris, 2011, Chart C5.2.

35   Danish Ministry of Education, 'Adult Vocational Training' at http://eng.uvm.dk/education-and-continuing-training/Adult-vocational-training.

36   Calculations made by comparing the Danish Ministry of Education's statistics with the data for the population aged 18 and above in the relevant year as reported by Statistics Denmark.

show the depth of ongoing adult learning and skills upgrading in Denmark. Skills training has for some time been in the Ministry of Education, though in close liaison with the Ministry of Employment. Training providers are required to have practical work and life experience in relevant fields to prepare for being well-suited to the specific requirements of adult teaching and learning.

The further education and skill enhancement of adults in Denmark is primarily coordinated by VEU centres. VEU is short in the Danish language for *Voksen-og EfterUddannelse*, meaning adult education and training. There are thirteen regionally designated VEU centres to coordinate the various educational institutions and on-the-job training providers. The AMU courses overseen by the VEUs are intensive, and full-time. The courses emphasise the importance of upskilling workers, e.g. unemployed former road construction workers, to improve their general skills in language expression and mathematics as well as more specific, vocationally oriented competencies. Among the roles of the VEU centres is to ensure that persons who need training in particular specialisations do go to the places, such as particular vocational and technical colleges, where there is actual expertise in teaching those specialisations. These specialisations may be in kitchen, hotel, restaurant, bakery or confectionery industry skills; gardening/horticulture; metalwork; welding and heating techniques; carpentry; technical installations and energy; administration; dairy and agriculture; transport; or the social and healthcare fields.[37] The coordination role played by the VEU centres ensures that vocational and technical colleges are not cut off from other parts of the broader Danish national educational network. This is in contrast to the

---

37   Interview with Jens Jacob Bødker, Head of Operations at Næstved VEU Centre, Denmark.

precarious position of TAFE colleges in Australia, especially after the severe public funding cuts to them and the pushing of them towards reliance on private sources of funding. The emphasis given to training by Denmark's Social Democrat-led government since it was elected in 2011 has been positive for the role of the VEU centres.

Denmark has an orientation to on-the-job practical training. Therefore, those, for example, who are training to be an assistant nurse spend most of the time in the hospital itself working while they are learning. Then they attend classes to learn the basics about medicine, anatomy, hygiene and related knowledge. The Danish vocational training approach is a practically oriented combination of practice and theory which does not over-emphasise classroom teaching and mostly involves hands-on work with relevant vocational equipment.[38]

Denmark also, very importantly, emphasises the *recognition of prior learning* and experience to add to classroom-type learning in order to give certified new qualifications. Educational institutions assess and acknowledge what Danish workers have already done. Thus labourers who have years' experience in working with bricklayers can gain credit for that experience, and the knowledge and skills which they acquired during it, towards the completion of adult apprenticeships to become bricklayers themselves. Those who have been working in a low-skilled job in a steel factory for several years and would like to move up to a more highly-skilled position which is in greater demand, such as a blue-collar industrial operator, will be given formal recognition for the competencies which they have gained for the new job during the previous on-the-job training which

---

38   Hendeliowitz interview.

they have, in effect, done. This shortens the period required to fulfil the more theoretical school component of their upgrading of skills to a diploma or other level.

Denmark has an extensive adult apprenticeship program which provides approximately 8,000 places a year, of which one-third are taken up by people previously unemployed. The program consists of a hiring subsidy for companies which employ an adult over 25 years of age in order to provide them with suitable vocational education. The aim is that lower-skilled workers, who did not receive sufficient education when they were young, can receive a vocational education. The employer pays the salary of the apprentice and receives a subsidy for the first two years of the apprenticeship period, which is normally four years. One condition of receiving the subsidy is that the training contract must be with a person over 25 years of age. Another is that the person either does not have vocational education, or has vocational education which has not been used during the preceding five years. Alternatively, there is a condition that the person has been on unemployment benefits or social assistance for more than nine months – for people aged 30 or over – or six months, in the case of those under 30. There is also a condition that the apprentice, during the period that the subsidy is paid, receives a salary at least equal to the lowest wage to which a low-skilled worker in the same sector is entitled. Approximately 40 per cent of Denmark's adult apprentices are aged between 25 and 29; while approximately 60 per cent are aged 30 years or more. Sixty per cent are low-skilled, while 40 per cent are more highly skilled or have a higher education prior to their entering the program to change career direction. Recent evaluation indicates that insured unemployed and social assistance recipients who are trained as adult apprentices have a high probability of finding a job in the first year after graduation.[39] To strengthen and further focus adult apprenticeships is one of the recommendations to build on Denmark's active labour market policy successes made by the Danish Government Expert Committee which reported in February 2014.[40]

The *Løntilskud* and *Virksomhedspraktik* job training programs, which range in length from four weeks to six months (with a possible extension to twelve months), are regulated by the Danish Agency for Labour Market and Recruitment as work experience or internship-type opportunities. The programs are subsidised by the municipalities and the state.[41] These are supported by Danish trade unions as they have positive effects for participants, including establishing or re-establishing unemployed people's structured work habits and routines, improving their networks along with their social skills, and boosting their confidence. At the same time, there are concerns to ensure that these programs do not become bases for cheap labour and displace existing actual paid jobs.[42]

There remains a constant tug of war in Denmark between employers and unions over whether flexibility or security is more important in 'Flexicurity'. There is a similar tug of war between Right-of-centre and Left-of-centre governments. Thus the former Right-of-centre government in 2010 made a decision which took effect in 2012 to reduce the unemployment benefit duration from a maximum of four

---

39   Per Kongshøj Madsen, 'European Employment Policy Observatory Review: Stimulating Job Demand: The Design of Effective Hiring Subsidies in Europe: Denmark', Centre for Labour Market Research, Aalborg, 2014, pp. 6–7.

40   *Veje til Job*, p. 9.

41   Interview with Helle Ekemann Jensen, Senior Adviser, Ministry of Employment, Denmark.

42   Interview with David Hedegaard Andersen, Adviser on Employment and Education, and Steen Jørgensen, Economist, Danish LO.

to a maximum of two years. This reduced the security component of 'Flexicurity'. The Social-Democrat-led government elected in 2011 has not reversed this as it does not have a parliamentary majority to do so. The Social Liberal Party, which is part of its current coalition government, was part of the previous parliamentary majority voting for the change. However, when, in 2012 and 2013, a large number of unemployed people lost their rights to insurance benefits because of the new policy, the current government provided a series of special payments to assist parents who were affected, and to support educational activities for others who were affected, as part of helping to tide them over.[43] This demonstrates Denmark's reluctance to actually move towards harsher policies towards the unemployed.

Danish employers, too, although they supported the reduction in the duration of the unemployment benefit, have not attacked the benefit *level*. Employers still broadly support 'Flexicurity' as it operates in Denmark, from which they receive the benefit of more skilled workers and the subsidies to train them (in addition of course to their flexibility to hire and fire). Thus the tug of war in Denmark takes place within clear limits. The embedded participation by, and contact between, employers and unions in Denmark on many issues also gives more capacity for work time sharing arrangements to be negotiated as an alternative to the retrenchment of workers than there is in countries which have less such participation and contact. The interaction between employers and unions also allows for innovations such as the 'Job Rotation' program.

In the Job Rotation program, one or more employees in an organisation participates in supplementary education while an unemployed

---

43   Information supplied by David Hedegaard Andersen, sourced from Danish Budget and Ministry of Employment documents.

person or persons temporarily carry out their work tasks. This enables employees to upgrade their skills and the unemployed to obtain training and experience through a temporary job. Frequently, Job Rotation program workers are hired after participating. Employers pay for the education of their own employees. They are compensated for hiring a Job Rotation program worker with the highest rate of unemployment benefits, plus 60 per cent for public employers and 80 per cent for private employers. The Job Rotation workers are hired at the normal wages and working conditions for the position which they fill for a temporary period. The program is focused on lower-skilled workers who have been unemployed for at least three months. They must be hired for at least ten hours a week, for a maximum of twelve months. It is very important to find the right match between the employers and the unemployed Job Rotation workers. Therefore, job centres or unemployment funds have individual meetings with possible candidates to make this match. The Job Rotation program improves the overall skills of the labour force while connecting unemployed people with paid employment opportunities. A regional evaluation of the Job Rotation program suggests that it increases the probability of unemployed people becoming self-supporting by as much as 20 percentage points.[44]

An estimated 8,000 direct and indirect jobs were lost in southern Denmark when the Lindø shipyard, owned by the Maersk company and located in the city of Odense, was closed in early 2012. The policy response taken by the Danish government has been suppor-tive of the workers' futures, as it was when shipbuilding operations

---

44 Danish LO materials provided by David Hedegaard Andersen. See also comments by Professor Henning Jørgensen from CARMA at Aalborg University quoted in *Nordic Labour Journal*, Work Research Institute, Oslo, May 2013, p. 14.

closed in Nakskov in the 1980s. The intention has been to try to preserve employees' skills in the local area and to redirect those into the development of large-scale renewable energy. Denmark has a Business Innovation Fund whose purpose is 'to promote growth, employment and export by supporting business opportunities within green growth and welfare as well as providing support for change-over to...[take advantage of] new business and growth opportunities in less favoured areas of the country'. The Fund focuses on 'large, cross-funded innovation programs...through grants and guarantees to firms'. From this Fund, southern Denmark received 37 million Danish kroner ($6.9 million) to develop the area where the shipyard is located 'into a brand new Lindø Renewable Energy Centre with incubation facilities for start-ups, a test centre, and other facilities that can attract new businesses and job opportunities...in renewable energy to the area'.[45] The Danish national government supplements money provided by the European Globalisation Adjustment Fund to help fund vocational training for, and reskilling of, the retrenched Lindø shipyard workers. The renewable energy plans for the region focus on wind turbine production and operation. The many wind turbines visible on the horizon, looking in all directions, in many parts of Denmark, are positive environmentally, in addition to their considerable job-creating benefits. The construction and installation of new wind turbines in the Danish part of the North Sea is one of several major infrastructure projects on which Denmark is now embarking as part of further reducing its reliance on fossil energy sources. Many former Lindø workers will be well-suited to work on that project. Official government websites indicate that Danish companies have, to date,

---

45   *OECD Reviews of Regional Innovation: Central and Southern Denmark 2012*, p. 109.

installed more than 90 per cent of the world's offshore wind turbines; that 28 per cent of the Danish electricity system is now supplied by wind power; and that the government aims to raise this to 50 per cent by the year 2020 as part of continuing Denmark's world-leading role in using the inexhaustible natural resource of wind power to help meet people's energy needs.[46] In its regeneration of the shipyard premises, as one researcher describes it: 'the partnership approach taken in Lindø by the municipalities, the unemployment benefit insurance funds, and also the private initiative around that place, has shown how you can redevelop a site that seemed doomed'.[47]

Other major infrastructure projects now planned in Denmark include: six state-of-the art hospitals; upgrading and improving the national railway system with high-speed connections; expanding the Copenhagen metropolitan train network; modernising and expanding the national highway system; and building a road and rail tunnel from the south-east of the country to Germany. These investments, together with the North Sea wind turbines, amount to 200 billion Danish kroner ($37.2 billion) and are expected to create 150,000 jobs in the next ten years. Just as importantly, serious efforts through customised programs are being made to *match* former Lindø shipyard workers, and other retrenched workers, to as many as possible of the new jobs which these investments will generate.[48] Another recommendation made by the Danish Government Expert Committee on labour market policy which reported in February 2014 is for 'annual early overviews of ongoing and forthcoming infrastructure projects

46   See: http://denmark.dk/en/green-living/wind-energy/.
47   Interview with Christian Lyhne Ibsen, Employment Relations Research Centre, University of Copenhagen.
48   *Ekspertudvalget vedrørende Infrastrukturinvesteringer og Arbejdskraft og Kvalifikationsbehov*, Danish Ministry of Employment, Copenhagen, 2013.

and other large construction works', and the implementation of 'a regional fund for job-targeted upgrading of qualifications' which are specifically 'adapted to the demands related to [those] infrastructure projects'.[49] Infrastructure projects are also linked to the maintenance and upgrading of people's skills in Denmark through formal requirements that if companies bid for a big construction project, their workers must have certificates of training to a level which matches national quality standards. Extensive privatisations and deregulations have tended to undermine Australia's capacity to insist on similar requirements. They have also drastically reduced the size of the public sector, which used to provide jobs and skills training for many people in a manner that Denmark's public sector still does.

The Lindø regeneration project provides an imaginative example of great interest for the future – and for the possible transition – of Victoria's La Trobe Valley, and other parts of Australia which have traditionally produced energy from non-renewable resources, such as the coal-mining centres of the Hunter Valley in New South Wales. There is no reason why the engineering and other skills previously used to manufacture cars in Australia could not be adapted, for instance, towards the manufacture of more wind turbines. There are also possibilities for building up in Australia the manufacturing needed for biomass, geothermal and other forms of renewable energy. Australia may not have the natural advantages of abundant wind in as many places as Denmark does. However, it does have a much greater natural advantage of sunlight than most countries, including some countries which have already developed solar power far more extensively. Australia can create economic, employment

---

49   *Veje til Job*, pp. 9, 10.

and environmental benefits from further large-scale initiatives to capture and utilise solar power in particular locations. These can add to the more than one million Australian households which have now installed photovoltaic panels.

Such initiatives can be part of meeting the huge potential for further rapid growth in renewable energy production which has been identified as feasible and preferable for Australia to meet the nation's future energy needs.[50] To achieve this growth, however, will require Australia to reaffirm, and then adhere to, a clear and ambitious Renewable Energy Target. Achieving the growth will also require Australia to get back in step with international efforts to price carbon.

A number of other manufacturing possibilities have been identified, with agreement from both unions and employers, as having growth prospects in Australia. These are: making machinery for the mining and construction sectors, and transport equipment for the aerospace industry; increased activity in defence supply chains and marine engineering; and the further development of Australia's urban and regional infrastructure.[51] The skills of displaced automotive and other workers should now be linked with these potential growth areas as a matter of urgent priority.

Denmark's Lindø project illustrates, more generally, how Australia should now, similarly, prepare to support, preserve and continue to utilise, as well as to renew and upgrade for national benefit, the skills and experience of its automotive and other manufacturing workers, instead of discarding them. One of the ways this should occur is

50   Ben Elliston, Iain MacGill and Mark Diesendorf, 'Least Cost 100 per cent Renewable Electricity Scenarios in the Australian National Electricity Market', *Energy Policy*, Vol. 59, August 2013, pp. 270–282.

51   *Prime Minister's Manufacturing Taskforce: A Report of the Non-Government Members*, Commonwealth of Australia, Canberra, August 2012, pp. 2, 5, 4.

through place-based initiatives for displaced workers concentrated in particular geographic areas disproportionately affected by industrial change.

A recent report by a government advisory body in Australia has found that more than 45 per cent of manufacturing workers do not have post-school qualifications, yet these are required by nearly 90 per cent of jobs in the industry. Better skills are clearly required for Australian manufacturing to enter additional high-tech, niche markets. Manufacturing may have a future in Australia, but the skills and qualifications of manufacturing workers will need to be adapted as part of this future being realised. The report recommends 'strategies that assist workers to transition to new roles, in combination with assistance packages'. It also recommends 'recognition of prior learning' in a way that assists manufacturing workers 'to identify and formally recognise the...skills and expertise', which they have built up during their working lives so far. Demand will increase in the future for science, technology, engineering and maths skills, so these abilities in particular need to be built up.[52] Many workers in the manufacturing sector in Australia will thus benefit from advanced programs of the kind which already operate in Denmark, including those which emphasise improvement of skills in language expression and mathematics.

The Danish government is continung to increase investment in education and training for the unemployed. This marks a clear contrast between the constructive Danish approach to supporting the unemployed into new jobs, and an ever-harsher and more dismissive Australian policy direction.

---

52   Australian Workforce and Productivity Agency, *Manufacturing Workforce Study*, Australian Government, Canberra, 2014, pp. 16, 13, 15.

Australia can learn from Danish-style 'Flexicurity', and from the skills enhancement, activating labour market program and employment services supports which have long been provided in Denmark for the unemployed. By doing so, Australia can provide successful training transitions for many 'prime-age' or 'mature-age' workers who have lost their previous jobs in industries such as manufacturing. This training can be for longer periods, and the upskilling can in particular cases be more fundamental, than has previously occurred or even been contemplated in Australia. The efforts put in by policy analysts and practitioners for Australia to learn and benefit from the Danish approach need now to be acted on. The detailed work which has been done towards a proper scheme of unemployment insurance for Australia, drawing from Danish experiences, needs now to be revisited, updated, fine-tuned and then championed for introduction. The Abbott government is abjectly failing to respond to the plight of mature-age unemployed workers. Its decision to extend work-for-the-dole projects indicates that it has no serious interest in providing quality skills training for the unemployed. The introduction in Australia of ALMPs and other training programs informed by Denmark's precedents can help provide a new, or renewed, set of skills for many of those workers. This will equip them to keep contributing their talents to add valuably to the output – as well as to meet the changing demands – of Australia's workforce.

Chapter 5

FOR THE PUBLIC GOOD: NORWAY'S COMPREHENSIVE TAXATION AND REGULATION OF NATURAL RESOURCE WEALTH

Norway's economy, like Australia's, relies heavily on the extraction of natural resources. However, unlike Australia, Norway has acted consistently to manage its natural resource endowments for the nation's long-term benefit.

The expanded mining and export of the extensive iron-ore deposits in the Pilbara area of Western Australia, and of bauxite, coal and other minerals, as well as the extraction of offshore oil and gas, came together to make up the first major private sector 'resources boom' in Australia during the 1960s. The Whitlam Labor Government, which was elected in 1972, tried to ensure that members of the Australian public gained a bigger share from this boom than they had under the Right-of-centre political parties which had been in office during the preceding decades. The Government exposed the inadequate taxation being paid by the private – mostly overseas-owned – mining companies, and it removed some of the tax concessions from which they had been excessively profiting. It sought greater public ownership of Australia's mineral and petroleum resources, and the development of more secondary industry in association with mining. The Whitlam Government also envisaged building a transcontinental pipeline network to move the liquefied natural gas (LNG), which had been discovered on Australia's north-west shelf to the centres with high demand for natural gas in Australia's south-east. This effort left some positive legacies, including a pipeline conveying gas from central Australia to Sydney and greater pursuit of the national interest by Australian governments in their dealings with mining companies than had been the case previously.[1] However, the policies became embroiled in, and tarnished by, the general political controversy over the 'Loans Affair' and the turbulent final year of the Whitlam Government in 1975. The failure to succeed in realising more of Labor's original ambitions before the international economic setbacks of the mid-1970s would cost Australia dearly.

At the same time, Norway established the basis for enduring national benefit from the rich oilfields which had recently been discovered in its territorial section of the North Sea. Norway's Labour Party was also elected to government in the early 1970s, with ideas for using state-owned companies to manage natural resources and for building up the nation's own industrial capacity. Supported by public servants, the government established substantial taxation of the international oil companies which came to drill in Norway's new North Sea oilfields. It also successfully created Statoil, a national,

---

1   Gough Whitlam, *The Whitlam Government 1972–1975*, Viking, Melbourne, 1985, pp. 249, 259, 250; Michael Sexton, *Illusions of Power: The Fate of a Reform Government*, Allen and Unwin, Sydney, 1979, pp. 95, 106; and Gary Smith, 'Minerals and Energy' in Alan Patience and Brian Head (eds.), *From Whitlam to Fraser: Reform and Reaction in Australian Politics*, Oxford University Press, Melbourne, 1979, pp. 233–241.

publicly owned oil company which took a 50 per cent ownership share of all new oilfields. Cross-party support ensured the continuation of these policies by later governments, led by different political parties, which soon followed.

Indeed, in 1972, Norway's parliament *unanimously* adopted a set of basic principles for the development of oil. These principles included that 'national supervision and control must be ensured for all operations on the NCS (Norwegian Continental Shelf)' and that 'petroleum discoveries must be exploited in a way which makes Norway as independent as possible of others for its supplies of crude oil'. Further, 'new industry will be developed on the basis of petroleum' and 'the development of an oil industry must take necessary account of existing industrial activities'. In addition, the Norwegian parliament unanimously determined that 'the state must become involved at all appropriate levels and contribute to a coordination of Norwegian interests in Norway's petroleum industry as well as the creation of an integrated oil community which sets its sights both nationally and internationally'.

In a far-sighted declaration, the parliament also declared that 'the development of an oil industry must take necessary account of…the protection of nature and the environment'.[2]

The unanimity achieved for these objectives in Norway in the early 1970s may have been because there were no private petroleum companies operating in Norway when the first North Sea oil discovery was made. This meant that there was no obvious business constituency to prod Right-of centre political parties into opposing plans for extensive government involvement in the oil industry. There was

---

2   Quoted in Bjørn Vidar Lerøen, '10 Commanding Achievements: The Norwegian Oil Model' in Bjørn Rasen (ed.), *Norwegian Continental Shelf: A Journal from the Norwegian Petroleum Directorate*, Vol. 7, No. 2, 2010, Norwegian Petroleum Directorate, Stavanger, pp. 11–13.

also broad acceptance of the principle that the oil belonged to the nation. Employers were divided on many other issues between more Right-wing sections (notably shipowners) and moderate industrialists (including the Norsk Hydro company) who saw themselves as part of Norwegian society, accepting its tripartite arrangements and associated responsibilities. Yet both stood to gain from the policy direction Norway took on natural resources then. The shipowners moved fast to take advantage of the opportunities for transitioning their own industry into new activities such as the building of oil rigs.[3]

The agreed cross-party approach to developing resources in Norway contrasted starkly with the polarised party politics of Australia in the 1970s. Norway's initial royalty-based tax arrangements for resources were adjusted in 1974 to ensure that they kept up with the actual extent of profit being made from resource extraction.[4] In Australia, by contrast, resources continued to be taxed in a way that was fragmented, very complex and varied widely between the states and territories. These tax arrangements were inefficient, and they were not equipped to keep up with – and hence they only captured a comparatively very small fraction of – growth in private mining company profits.

Norway's decision-makers also adopted an interventionist policy to develop the nation's transport and infrastructure, together with the expansion of the oil industry. This included construction and operation of what would become a large and elaborate network of pipelines.[5] The government acted for Norway to develop and use new

3   Interview with Helge Ryggvik.
4   Helge Ryggvik, *The Norwegian Oil Experience: A Toolbox for Managing Resources?*, Centre for Technology, Innovation and Culture, University of Oslo, Oslo, 2010, p. 51.
5   Ibid. pp. 24–26, 28; and Yngvild Tormodsgard (ed.), *Facts 2014: The Norwegian Petroleum Sector*, Norwegian Ministry of Petroleum and Energy, Oslo, and Norwegian Petroleum Directorate, Stavanger, 2014, pp. 18–19, 21.

technologies which were capable of handling the rough conditions of the North Sea. Norwegian companies involved in manufacturing, engineering, information and communications technology, and business services, helped by supportive government policies, expanded their sales in the large markets which the new oil and gas industry opened up.[6] Existing national expertise in the making and usage of concrete was adapted for the construction of major concrete storage tanks, and of concrete base structures to sit on the seabed in deep water to form the base of massive new oil platforms. These generated tens of thousands of Norwegian jobs. Later, Norsk Hydro adapted to be an oil company and introduced important incremental innovations into production-drilling platforms which were fabricated from steel.[7] Statoil helped to build up Norway's supplies to the oil industry and pursued a strong policy for Norwegian local content in industries related to oil and gas.

In Australia, trade unions and others have likewise long pushed for local content and for the development of other industries together with resource extraction. These efforts have not only been made in the mining industry. They have also been made in the North-West Shelf LNG project and in the production of oil and of liquid petroleum gas (LPG) in Bass Strait: both of which started at a similar time to Norway's oil production. However, efforts for local content, and for industrial development to build on resource extraction, have received notably less government support in Australia than they have in Norway.

---

6   See the introductory chapter of Jan Fagerberg, David Mowery and Bart Verspagen (eds.), *Innovation, Path Dependency, and Policy: The Norwegian Case*, Oxford University Press, Oxford, 2009, p. 7.

7   Ole Andreas Engen, 'The Development of the Norwegian Petroleum Innovation System: A Historical Overview' in Fagerberg, Mowery and Verspagen (eds.), *Innovation, Path Dependency, and Policy: The Norwegian Case*, pp. 192, 199, 195.

CHAPTER 5

Dr Helge Ryggvik, who has written extensively on the history of Norway's oil industry, describes how Statoil 'benefited from the fact that the Norwegian educational system…made great efforts to meet the new industry's needs' by reorienting itself to the possibilities which Norway's new-found natural resource wealth offered. The technical college in Trondheim, Norway, began training engineers with relevant qualifications. Further, 'as students saw their own prospects, Statoil was the top choice for starting a career. Within the geology departments at the universities of Oslo and Bergen, the emphasis in teaching and research was rapidly shifted from the bedrock which characterised dry land in Norway to the kind of sedimentary rocks where oil was to be found'. One of many companies which benefited considerably from the policy to support Norwegian industry was Petroleum Geo Services, which today supplies advanced seismic services worldwide.[8] Statoil also insisted that major components of research relevant to the oil industry be carried out in Norway. Support by the Norwegian government for research and development in areas related to the expanding resource extraction industry led to the development of considerable local research expertise in applied geology, well-drilling technology, oil recovery and the transportation of fluids from oilfields.[9]

Norway now has many technologically advanced, world-leading companies with expertise in drilling and underwater infrastructure. Co-operative tripartite organisation financially supported by the Norwegian government keeps up collaboration between the public and private sectors in the development and export from Norway of

8   Ryggvik, *The Norwegian Oil Experience*, pp. 42, 62.
9   Engen, 'The Development of the Norwegian Petroleum Innovation System', pp. 194, 201.

products developed in association with oil extraction.[10] These exports include platform decks and drilling packages.[11]

Norway's expertise is recognised by, among others, the chief executive of a major engineering and project services company which has long worked with the mining industry in Western Australia. Mr Kevin Gallagher, from the Clough Corporation, praises the Norwegian government for the way that it 'in 1972 implemented policies encouraging...partnering with local technology companies and specialist engineering companies to develop those skills in Norway'. He also praises the results, which include the fact that 'Norway today is an exporter of...strategically critical skills', having as many as '50 service providers listed on the Norwegian stock exchange with a...cumulative market cap of around $50 billion'. Along with other leaders of companies connected to the resource industry, Gallagher believes that it is still possible for Australia to take its own action to achieve greater local technological development and innovation.[12] The challenge is for Australia to do more than it currently does with the extraction of its natural resources, to invest so as to create exportable skills that will help sustain its economy beyond the boom, like Norway but unlike other countries, including Britain, which have handled their resource wealth in a very short-term way. In contrast to Norway, Britain notoriously frittered away much of the riches which it extracted from its own, neighbouring share of North Sea oil, particularly through its handing out of tax cuts to the well-off during the Thatcher years.

10   *INTSOK Norwegian Oil and Gas Partners 2013 Annual Report*, INTSOK, Oslo, Stavanger and Bergen, 2013, p. 2 and *passim*.
11   Tormodsgard (ed.), *Facts 2014: The Norwegian Petroleum Sector*, p. 56.
12   Comments made on ABC television program *The Business*, 13 November 2012.

After the fall of the Whitlam Government, the ALP officially continued, up until 1988, with a policy for a publicly owned entity (an 'Australian Hydrocarbons Corporation') to participate in the development of Australia's oil and gas resources and to act itself as an oil company. However, this policy – which would have created an organisation like Norway's Statoil – was not implemented by the Hawke Labor Government, which turned instead to the pursuit of privatising and deregulatory economic policies. The Hawke Government did, however, introduce a Petroleum Resource Rent Tax (PRRT) in 1987. It could do this because the national government had clear jurisdiction over off-shore resources, whereas taxation of on-shore *mineral* deposits continued to be determined by elaborate arrangements varying between the states and territories. Because petroleum makes up a much smaller share of Australia's overall resource extraction than it does of Norway's, Australia's overall resources industry remained very lightly taxed compared to Norway's.

In 1990, in recognition of the greatly increased size of the oil industry, and its particularly large proportional importance for Norway's economy, the Norwegian government took new action to regulate revenues from oil so that that they would not be spent irresponsibly. The government formed the Petroleum Fund, into which money began to be deposited in 1996. In 2006 this became the Government Pension Fund – Global (*Statens Pensjonsfond*). It is commonly referred to by Norwegians as the *Oljefondet* (Oil Fund), while it is often referred to in other parts of the world as Norway's 'sovereign wealth fund'. The fund is fully owned by the Norwegian state through the Ministry of Finance. It is managed by Norway's central bank (Norges Bank). It has grown to be worth more than

5,000 billion Norwegian kroner.[13] This equals more than $800 billion. The fund takes in all the considerable revenues which the government receives from Norway's oil and gas, including taxes, ownership shares, and dividends from Statoil. It then invests these outside Norway, in order to prevent adverse effects from those revenues on the nation's currency exchange rate and therefore on the Norwegian economy.

A major review of Australia's future tax system – which I will call hereafter the Henry Tax Review, after its chair, the then Treasury Secretary Ken Henry – was commissioned in 2008, and it issued its final report (the Henry Report) in 2009.[14] One of the papers prepared for this review (though not publicly released until later) identified how in Norway, 'the Government Pension Fund – Global is used to invest revenue from mining with two main stated aims'. The first is 'to ensure petroleum revenues are available for use by future generations as well as current generations' so as 'to provide the government with savings on which to draw in periods where public disbursements are too large to be financed by tax'. The second is to separate 'current petroleum revenues' from 'the use of these revenues in the economy' in order 'to shield the economy from fluctuations in prices and extraction rates in the petroleum sector'. This second aim is in line with the principle, well-established among economists, that nations with substantial natural resources need to manage these in a way which prevents the nation's currency from rising to the extent of disadvantaging other sectors of the national economy. In Norway,

---

13   See the relevant section of the Norwegian Ministry of Finance web site at
     http://www.regjeringen.no/en/dep/fin/Selected-topics/the-government-pension-
     fund/market-value-of-the-government-pension-f.html?id=699635.

14   Australian Government, *Australia's Future Tax System: Report to the Treasurer December 2009, Overview*, Commonwealth of Australia, Canberra, 2010.

as the Australian authors of the Henry Tax Review working paper also noted, the use of the sovereign wealth fund 'is limited to four per cent, or the expected annual real return on the...fund over time... This rule is to ensure use of the revenues can be sustained over time. The government sees that the fund is not savings but represents the conversion of petroleum wealth to financial investments'.[15] A proportion of those investments can then be used by the national government each year.

Accordingly, Norwegian governments receive the benefit of up to 4 per cent of – or the expected annual real return on – the Government Pension Fund's investments, each year, for their budgeting. At the same time, the fund stays overwhelmingly intact and growing for the future.

Australia's lack of a coherent national minerals tax led to clear problems for the non-mining sectors of the economy in the new resources boom which developed in the 2000s. These problems were particularly felt by the manufacturing sector, whose exports became much more expensive because of the high dollar which Australia's latest resources boom fuelled.

It was in this context that the first Rudd Labor Government, in its May 2010 budget, announced plans for a new 40 per cent Resource Super Profits Tax. The plans were in line with a specific recommendation to consolidate and update resources taxation in Australia, which had been made by the panel which prepared the Henry Report. That panel included the chief executive of the Australian Industry Group. The proposed new Resource Super Profits Tax aimed to

---

15 Lindsay Hogan and Rebecca McCallum, *Non-Renewable Resource Taxation in Australia*, Australian Bureau of Agricultural and Resource Economics – Bureau of Rural Sciences (ABARE-BRS) Report prepared for the Australia's Future Tax System Review Panel, ABARE-BRS, Canberra, 2010, p. 15.

rectify the fact that Australia had been deprived of much valuable revenue, to which it was entitled, because of insufficient taxation of the hugely escalating mining companies' profits. Government documents reported how,

> over the recent period of rising resource prices the community's share in the increased value of its deposits, received through existing resource taxes and royalties, has been declining...The effective resource charge (charges as a percentage of super profits earned) has more than halved from an average of around 34 per cent over the first half of this decade to less than 14 per cent in 2008–2009. Existing resource taxes and royalties have only delivered a small share of the increased value of resource deposits. Resource profits were over $80 billion higher in 2008–2009 than in 1999–2000, but governments only collected an additional $9 billion through resource charges.[16]

Now Australia seemed to be learning something from Norway. Indeed, during the debate on this proposed new tax for Australia, Ken Henry as secretary of the treasury, at a Senate budget estimates committee hearing, explicitly pointed to Norway as still attracting very substantial amounts of private capital investment, despite taking a far higher proportion of the profits than Australia's proposed tax would.[17] The report by the Henry Review of taxation referred to how Norway's resource charging system had played an important role in supporting petroleum exploration and development in that nation. The Australian Government's 2010 policy announcement followed

---

16   Australian Government, *2010-11 Australian Government Budget – Budget Paper No. 1*, Commonwealth of Australia, Canberra, 2010, Statement 4; Australian Government, *The Resource Super Profits Tax: A Fair Return to the Nation*, Commonwealth of Australia, Canberra, 2010, p. 10.

17   Commonwealth of Australia, Official Committee Hansard Senate Economics Legislation Committee Estimates (Budget Estimates), Canberra, Thursday, 27 May 2010, p. 25.

the Henry report in identifying how 'Norway imposes a total tax rate on resource super profits of 78 per cent, consisting of a 50 per cent super profit based tax rate and company income tax of 28 per cent, with no deduction at the company tax level for payments of the super profit based tax'.[18]

Therefore, the hostile and threatening campaign which was then unleashed by mining companies during 2010, which suggested that Australia was trying to move to the world's highest tax on resources, was highly misleading. The companies did not include petroleum, as well as minerals, in their international tax comparisons. Yet Australia's Labor Government was unable to mobilise support for its original tax plan. This was due in part to it not appealing strongly enough to egalitarian arguments and to not adequately highlighting relevant evidence from international precedents.

The Resource Super Profits Tax policy proposal of 2010 was also caught up in, and undermined by, the machinations of a very divided Labor Party leadership. The merits of the proposal were very weakly communicated by the government.[19]

Just as some mining companies in Australia threatened to end their operations in Australia after 2010 unless the government bowed to their opposition to paying the proposed new tax, so international oil companies have attempted similar tactics against Norway. The privately owned American petroleum company Phillips, for example, following the 1969 discovery of the first major oilfield in the Norwegian section of the North Sea, vigorously protested the

---

18   Australian Government, *The Resource Super Profits Tax: A Fair Return to the Nation*, p. 11.

19   David McKnight and Mitchell Hobbs, 'Public Contest through the Popular Media: The Mining Industry's Advertising War against the Australian Labor Government', *Australian Journal of Political Science*, Vol. 48, No. 3, 2013, pp. 315–316.

decision by Statoil to itself be the main owner and controller of oil pipelines in Norway, rather than to give Phillips that strategicially important role. However,

> at the end of the day, Phillips calculated that there was so much oil in the...field that it would nevertheless produce large profits...Norway...thus experienced for the first time how foreign companies could use a combination of lobbying and power to establish positions which were apparently reasonable and unshakeable, but which [in fact] could be challenged by a comparable counter-power.[20]

Likewise, when the tax changes were made in 1974, Phillips and other major oil companies protested angrily but 'the Norwegian Ministry of Finance...did not let itself be scared off. Its underlying understanding was...[that] the state had to aim for the greatest possible share of the economic' benefit from large oilfields 'to go to the community'. Further, the Ministry correctly judged that, 'as long as the oil companies secured profits which corresponded to, or were higher than, those in other industries', then they would continue their operations.[21] The Australian government from 2010 to 2012 should have similarly recognised the mining companies' threats as not being credible. It should have similarly stood firm to rebuff those threats.

Instead, with the watering down of the original proposed 2010 Resource Super Profits Tax into the 2012 Minerals Resource Rent Tax (MRRT), a much lesser amount was envisaged for collection; and very little at all was initially collected. Yet there remains potential for continuing taxation of mining for national benefit in Australia. The Abbott Government's decision to axe the MRRT will needlessly

20   Ryggvik, *The Norwegian Oil Experience*, p. 30.
21   Ibid. p. 52.

forego further potential revenue, mostly from overseas-owned resource companies, to which Australia as a whole is entitled – and which could be used for very many, socially useful expenditure purposes. In Norway, meanwhile, international private sector oil companies, including BP and ExxonMobil, are continuing to operate profitably in a taxation and regulatory situation which some Australian commentary has quite wrongly portrayed as impossibly prohibitive.

Statoil's scope was limited in 1985, with bi-partisan support, to prevent it from becoming an excessive centre of power. Half of the Norwegian government's direct involvement in the petroleum industry has since then been managed by a separate state holding company called Petoro, which since 2001 has been located in the bustling oil town of Stavanger, in the country's south-west. Another important official organisation formed in the early 1970s which has been built up to regulate, and provide expert independent analysis of, the oil industry is the Norwegian Petroleum Directorate.

Statoil is also now – following a series of changes since 2001 – one-third privatised. This reflects the partial influence of the neo-liberal economic ideas which resurged around the world from the 1980s but which reached into the Nordic nations to a much lesser extent than they did into the English-speaking nations. Although any idea of state-owned oil companies may seem very radical and alien in English-speaking countries today, BP (British Petroleum) was itself mostly state-owned until the Thatcher government fully privatised it in 1987. Today, the still majority government-owned Statoil continues to play a crucial and efficient part in Norway's participation in the international energy industry, in a way that brings rewards to Norwegian society. The proceeds from Norway's taxation and regulation of resource wealth also contribute to the continuation of another policy which too many people in Australia regard as unrealistic and needing to be discarded since the 1970s but which in Norway remains entirely affordable: free university education.

Norway's Global Pension Fund operates according to highly ethical principles. It has removed investments from companies which are involved with tobacco, weapons production, or which have caused environmental damage. The Norwegian parliament is also currently considering removing the Fund's investments from coal, because of coal's heavily polluting effects.

These policies continue Norway's role as an environmentally responsible nation. This role is closely associated with the international contribution made by Norway's former Labour prime minister, Gro Harlem Brundtland. She became Norway's first female prime minister in 1981 and was prime minister again from 1986 to 1989 and from 1990 to 1996. Her only ministerial position prior to becoming prime minister was as Minister for the Environment. Following her first stint as prime minister, she headed the World Commission on the Environment and Development which was formed by the United Nations in 1983, and which in 1987 published the landmark report titled *Our Common Future*. Gro Harlem Brundtland's personal perspective on environmental issues was shaped by her early experiences seeing inequalities in America, and her work as a medical doctor and then as a public health researcher. She recognised from a young age how important environmental protection is for people's health, especially for the health of people experiencing socio-economic disadvantage. She also recognised early the need to connect environmental policies with economic policies. Brundtland writes in her memoirs about how important it was for her that ecological agendas were pursued not only in the Ministry of the Environment but also in 'the Ministries of Finance and Energy' because only those ministries have the 'authority and budgets that can be applied so that they really make a difference'.[22] The pioneering role which Norway played in late 20th century efforts to enable employees to gain more control over their 'work environment' and the very notion and terminology of the 'work environment' (see page 27) similarly brought environmental issues into everyday economic life instead of treating 'the environment' as a separate and marginal concern.

Norway's position as a large oil producer – and the ambitions of some Norwegians to keep thrusting further northwards to find more oil beneath the sea – do create some tensions with its role as an environmentally responsible nation.[23] Nevertheless, in the urgent 21st century debates between countries about how to respond to environmentally threatening climate change by reducing greenhouse gas emissions, Norway remains a global leader. As Australian expert Robyn Eckersley writes: 'Norway's mitigation targets are radically more ambitious than Australia's and are among the highest in the world', whereas 'Australia's targets hover in the lower band of developed countries'. In part, she points out, this difference is because 'the climate discourses of Australian political leaders are much more fractured than those of their Norwegian counterparts'. In Australia, 'there is a much greater strain of climate denialism' in the major political parties, i.e. a refusal to accept the overwhelming scientific evidence of global warming and associated catastrophic

22   Gro Harlem Brundtland, *Madam Prime Minister: A Life in Power and Politics*, Farrar, Strauss and Giroux, New York, 2002, p. 198. See also pp. 18, 27, 42, 52, 89, 195, 200, 211, 226, 229, 268.

23   Ryggvik, *The Norwegian Oil Experience*, pp. 91–94; Robyn Eckersley, 'Poles Apart? The Social Construction of Responsibility for Climate Change in Australia and Norway', *Australian Journal of Politics and History*, Vol. 59, No. 3, 2013, pp. 386, 389, 390.

environmental trends. This – once again, as in many other areas of policy which have been discussed in this book – 'reflects a much more adversarial political culture' in Australia than exists in the Nordic nations.[24]

This lesser adversarialism exists in part because, in Norway, like Sweden – but unlike the Australian parliament and most parliaments in the world – seating is arranged according to the geographic constituencies which the members of parliament represent, not according to their party affiliation. Thus, parliamentarians from the same regions, but from different political parties, sit next to each other in the legislative chamber in Norway, and in Sweden. This arrangement reduces the tendency for all members of one political party to just congregate together and barrack, in a mindless way, against their opponents. It therefore makes it less likely for politicians to artificially exaggerate differences with opponents for short-term advantage. The parliamentary seating arrangement, instead, encourages discovery of areas where there might be agreement.

Norway's approach to taxation and regulation not only ensures that the nation's natural resources are used in an economically sustainable way. It also creates a basis of public financing support for major environmental projects. The Norwegian government announced in 2012 a new series of initiatives including to improve public transport in cities and larger towns by investing in railways; to recognise the importance of forests for countering carbon dioxide gases and therefore to preserve those forests; and to construct at least one full-scale demonstration facility for carbon capture and storage by 2020. Further, a Green Fund for Climate, Renewable Energy and Energy

24 Eckersley, 'Poles Apart?', p. 390.

Efficiency Measures was established to develop technology which better reduces greenhouse gas emissions. Government investment in this fund will rise to 50 billion Norwegian kroner ($8.3 billion) in 2020.[25]

It is tempting to see the Nordic variety of capitalist, who has a sense of being a responsible citizen and of observing some rules of civility in public debates, as entirely different from the more Texas oil-style 'frontier capitalists' who have become so prominent in the Australian resource extraction industry. Such individuals include billionaire Gina Rinehart, who was one of the most publicly prominent participants in the campaign against a fair mining tax from 2010 to 2012. She has expressed pride in her late father, Lang Hancock, who set up the iron-ore mining companies which she inherited. In an interview on a Brisbane television program on 5 October 1981, Lang Hancock said, in relation to indigenous Australians who are what he called half-castes, that he 'would dope the water up so they were sterile and would breed themselves out in future and that would solve the problem'.[26] Gina Rinehart also says some highly offensive things. For instance, she has told Australians that they need to work harder to compete with some workers overseas who receive less than $2 a day.[27] She is the subject of legal action by most of her children to gain any inheritance of their own, while her companies face fines for allegedly not lodging annual reports in breach of corporation law.

Support for greater taxation and regulation of Australia's huge mineral wealth, however, is not, however, confined to the political

---

25   'Ambitious Norwegian White Paper on Climate Efforts', Office of the Prime Minister, Press Release, Oslo, 26 April 2012.

26   Quoted in Debi Marshall, *Lang Hancock*, Allen and Unwin, Sydney, 2001, p. 139.

27   Reported on ABC Radio *AM* program, 5 September 2012.

Left. Some senior private sector leaders are among those who view the considerable dilution of the original proposed Resource Super Profits Tax of 2010 as the loss of a great public policy opportunity to use more of the massive profits made from Australia's latest resources boom to advance the national interest.

Several prominent Australian business leaders, meanwhile, have explicitly supported a Norwegian-style sovereign wealth fund. Former Commonwealth Bank chief executive Ralph Norris, for example, stated that: 'mining companies are recovering resources that are the natural endowment of Australians, and therefore Australia... should look to get some return'. Australia needs to look to Norway's government pension fund, built up from more than two decades of revenue from its share of the North Sea oilfields, he has said.[28] Malcolm Turnbull, who was a successful businessperson before entering the national parliament, and who lost his position as Leader of the Liberal Party in 2009 partly because of his willingness to give bi-partisan support to the Labor Government's then proposed emissions trading scheme, is a comparatively progressive minister in the Abbott Government. He is another person who has supported formation of a new sovereign wealth fund to improve Australia's long-term savings. Turnbull argues that Australia has squandered the fruits of every resources and primary produce boom in our history and that it is time to adopt a more mature approach.[29]

In 2006 the Australian government did form a Future Fund. This sounds good, and it is positive as far as it goes; but it receives no revenues from resource profits, and it is very narrowly cast to meeting future liabilities for the payment of some superannuation benefits

---

28   *The Age*, Melbourne, 18 February 2011.
29   Reported in *The Age*, Melbourne, and *The Sydney Morning Herald*, 8 April 2011.

to some retiring public servants. This fund's holdings amount to only one-tenth of Norway's fund holdings, even though Norway's population is little more than one-fifth the size of Australia's population. The Future Fund needs to be radically expanded into a full sovereign wealth fund if it is to play the far-sighted economic and social role for Australia, which the *Statens Pensjonsfond* has long been playing for Norway.

In a series of media interviews since he was freed from the constraints of being treasury secretary, Ken Henry has made clear statements about the need to increase taxation in Australia. He has said that both major political parties in Australia need to face up to the fact that they cannot deliver new services, and a budget surplus, without any increased taxes. If they do not face up to this reality, he says, then governments will have to keep cutting spending as a 'permanent process'. Australia instead needs to 'improve the tax system so it's capable of producing more revenue with minimal economic damage', he says; and, as part of that, it will still 'need to find ways to apply higher rates of tax to natural resources including mineral resources'.[30] Henry points out how the national government's revenue fell from 26 per cent of GDP in 2001 to just 23 per cent of GDP in 2013. He has said that: 'I certainly did not anticipate that today [national government] revenue would be 3 percentage points of Gross Domestic Product below where it was a little more than a decade ago'. Indeed, he describes it as 'incredible' that revenue could be that low given 'the fact that Australia has had such a strong resources boom' in that time. Over the same period, national government expenditure as a proportion of GDP fell from 25 per

30   *The Age*, Melbourne, and *The Sydney Morning Herald*, 6 August 2013.

cent to 24 per cent. It is 'because revenue has fallen by 3 percentage points of GDP and spending has fallen by only 1 per cent' that the national budget went from surplus to deficit, Dr Henry says.[31] The implication of this is clearly that governments should stop focusing on cutting government spending and start focusing on fair ways to increase government revenue.

Ken Henry also says that: 'If you ask me the question do we have the capacity to finance new spending without new sources of revenue, the answer is no'. He criticises the series of personal income tax cuts which were delivered by both the Howard and the Rudd governments for having put the budget under considerable pressure.[32]

If Australians are to receive more services, benefits and programs than they currently do, then the necessary revenue will need to be raised. A universal approach does cost considerable money. When national and state and territory government taxes for 2013 are combined together in an internationally comparable way, taxes in Australia amount to 33 per cent of GDP, which is the equal fourth lowest of 31 OECD nations. In each of the four main Nordic nations, in the same year, taxes are more than 50 per cent of GDP.[33] However, the high workforce participation produced by those countries' policies helps to generate the necessary taxation revenue. In addition to the high employment rates in the Nordic nations which I have previously mentioned, such as among women in Sweden (see page 87) and among 'prime-age' workers in Denmark (see pages 141–142), the Henry Report brings to light another group which participates at comparatively high rates in the paid workforce in all the Nordic

---

31   *The Age*, Melbourne, and *The Sydney Morning Herald*, 1 May 2014.
32   Transcript of interview on ABC television program *7.30*, 12 March 2014.
33   OECD, *OECD Economic Outlook 2013*, Statistical Annex, Table 26.

nations. The proportion of working-age people with *disabilities* who are in paid employment is above the OECD average of 43 per cent in each of the four main Nordic nations, whereas it languishes well below that average in Australia.[34]

The positive quality of the benefits, services and programs which are received by citizens of the Nordic nations, from the large revenue which their governments gain, leads, in turn, to their continued overall support for payment of the taxes. Universalism in welfare provision means that the middle class has a stake in the provision of services and is therefore prepared to pay the taxes necessary to support those services. By contrast, when benefits are limited only to the most vulnerable people as in the US, then the rest of the population feel that they are paying for something from which they do not receive anything in return, so they become even less likely to support paying taxes. The selective and minimal welfare arrangements which apply in America lead to a spiralling hostility towards some categories of welfare recipients.

The purist market liberal economic ideology which has predominated in the English-speaking countries since the 1980s is often, quite falsely, presented as if it is the only available option for nation states to follow. The Centre of Equality, Social Organisation, and Performance (ESOP), which is based at the University of Oslo in Norway, is one centre which counters this propaganda with detailed contrary evidence from Nordic experience. ESOP also explores the implications of that evidence for general economic thinking. The Centre's research seeks to explain how the Nordic nations have continued to achieve distinctive

---

34   Australian Government, *Australia's Future Tax System: Report to the Treasurer December 2009, Part Two, Detailed Analysis, Volume 2 of 2*, Commonwealth of Australia, Canberra, 2010, pp. 515–516.

economic, employment and innovation successes while maintaining, for instance, a central role for trade unions. Notwithstanding the interventionist industry policy associated with the rise of Norway's oil industry which I have outlined in this chapter, ESOP emphasises the Nordic nations' good credentials as open and prolifically trading economies. ESOP also considers the reasons that high taxes and an expansive welfare state can enhance, rather than constrain, economic prosperity.[35] Australia can learn a great deal from this line of enquiry as it seeks to shape its own financial future.

One reason Australia's revenue is so low is the large tax concessions given to property investors, which also make housing less affordable for more needy people. Another reason is the overly favourable and highly inequitable tax treatment of the superannuation of high-income earners. These and other specifically regressive taxation policies need to be changed. More generally, the shocking lack of *numeracy* and/or honesty from political leaders in Australia about the revenue reality and its implications needs to be challenged. It is damaging the nation now and into the future. Australia's existing meagre welfare provision – and further desirable provision – are only 'unsustainable' for as long as the current treasurer and other political leaders fail to work out how to add up – or publicly admit the need to add up – some very simple sums. Australia's taxation needs to now rise in order to match the expenditure which Australia needs to now make in order to become more economically, socially and environmentally successful.

The linking of new taxes to particular desired benefits, services or programs is one way to help to increase support for those taxes.

---

35 The publications and other output and activities of this Centre can be viewed at the following link: http://www.esop.uio.no/about/.

CHAPTER 5

The Medicare levy has always been an unusually popular 'tax' because payment of it is clearly linked to people's visits to doctors being more affordable. The welcome decision taken, with bi-partisan support, to increase this levy from 1.5 per cent to 2 cent of taxable income to fund the introduction of the new 'Disability Care' service is therefore an approach worth considering for other new services, benefits and programs in Australia which require financing.

In an incisive article, which fully faces the electoral difficulties of seeking increased taxation in the realities of Australian politics, Shaun Wilson nevertheless shows clearly that the 'low-tax social democracy' approach which the ALP has endeavoured to take since the time of the Whitlam Government 'has limited redistributive potential' and 'has reached its fiscal and political limits'. He also reports on 'research into public opinion' in order 'to identify opportunities...available to governments as they attempt to finance welfare' in Australia. He finds, from 2011 Australian National University polling data, that, when asked to choose between reducing taxes or spending more on social services, 60 per cent of voters prefer spending, compared with 37 per cent who prefer tax cuts. This reflects concerns about the way Australia's social infrastructure has been running down, to the detriment of future generations. When examined in more detail, this data shows that 'education attracts the highest preferences for more spending', with more than 80 per cent support. More spending on 'childcare' and 'families with low incomes' also attracts majority support, with the proportion supporting greater expenditure in those policy areas 'ranging from 52 per cent to 60 per cent'. The data also indicates 'strong support (60 per cent) for greater taxation of all three types of large businesses: carbon polluters, mining companies and banks', as part of a 'voter inclination to tax super profits'. Wilson further suggests that there is considerable electoral potential in Australia of a 'policy of raising taxes for higher income earners'.[36]

There are still egalitarian sentiments in Australia. More effective political leadership and judgement will be needed to channel these sentiments into policy change. Part of that leadership will involve disseminating better knowledge of the great economic, social and environmental benefits which increased revenue, well-spent, can bring.

The conflict over Australian resource tax policy from 2010 to 2012 demonstrated the difficulty of, on the one hand, giving incentives for private companies to search for and extract natural resources, and, on the other hand, gaining a fair return for the nation which owns those natural resources. Difficult though it is, this issue – and the urgent underlying revenue imperatives which pushed it to such political prominence in Australia – will not go away. Norway's success as a result of taking a different approach is particularly illuminating of how, and why, Australia should keep striving to strengthen its arrangements for resource taxation.

---

36   Shaun Wilson, 'The Limits of Low-Tax Social Democracy? Welfare, Tax and Fiscal Dilemmas for Labor in Government', *Australian Journal of Political Science*, Vol. 48, No. 3, 2013, pp. 291, 300, 293, 295, 296, 302.

CONCLUSION

At what is now a crucial time for the determination of Australia's future, the past interest shown by some Australians, and by some people from other English-speaking countries, in the policy achievements of Sweden and other Nordic nations needs to be reactivated. This interest also needs to reach into new realms of policy and to reach out to wider audiences, in order to realise more substantial policy change.

Policies pursued in the four main Nordic nations have achieved much lower levels of child poverty, better supports and services for parents when their children are young, better work/life balance, better school results, greater skills and job opportunities for workers still in their prime working years, and a sounder base of revenue for necessary government spending, including on environmental measures, than have been achieved in Australia and other English-speaking countries.

It is therefore unacceptable for Australian policy makers to keep ignoring the compelling evidence of how the Nordic nations are doing things differently, and more successfully, in so many vital areas of policy. The Nordic countries are real places. They are in the OECD group of developed countries comparable to Australia. They have not disappeared. Policy makers need to overcome irrational fears which prevent them from talking about places where taxes are higher and where workers' rights are better protected.

Further, no one should feel paralysed by the notion that it is too late, for Australia or other English-speaking nations, to do any of the things which the Nordic nations do, because the two groups of nations diverged forever as a result of previous steps taken decades ago. That is, no one should feel paralysed by the notion of 'path dependency', which was discussed on page 14. The ombudsman, children's commissioners, prohibition of physical violence against children, and paid parental leave are initiatives originating in the Nordic nations which have already been taken up in many other parts of the world. Take-up of further specific Nordic policy initiatives can follow. Finland's innovations over recent decades, meanwhile, confirm the *general* capacity which individual nation states still have to make major changes in policy direction.

To the extent that we do now live in more fluid 'globalised' times, it is appropriate that we take more, rather than less, interest in a wide range of international experiences, beyond the US, Britain, New Zealand and Canada, than previous generations did. Only by now broadening their international reference points can citizens in Australia and in other English-speaking countries gain full knowledge of other political and policy options which are available to shape their future.

In Australia, unquestionably, constituencies and influences will continue to be arrayed against social democratic policies of the kind characteristic of Nordic Europe. However, there are also large and powerful constituencies which are concerned about Australia's high and rising levels of economic inequality. Members of these constituencies are alarmed by the setback to egalitarianism which the imposition of neo-liberal policies has meant. They are now seeking policy alternatives. They can be effectively mobilised by policy actors who show more genuine curiosity and endeavour, and greater intellectual self-confidence, in drawing attention to proven alternatives to neo-liberalism. The case for adopting different policies is strengthened by showing how those policies are already working well in practice in some parts of the world, rather than just arguing the merits of those policies in theory.

It is significant that the expert health researchers who wrote the book *The Spirit Level* – arising out of their enquiries into what determines people's wellbeing – emphasise the importance of once again aiming for industrial democracy to make working life fairer and more fulfilling by employees having greater influence on the way they work.[1] That aim was one of the main reasons for the interest in Nordic Europe which arose among the earlier generations of Australian political activists, trade unionists and intellectuals who were discussed in Chapter 1.

The authors of *The Spirit Level* are among a range of experts from various disciplines – including epidemiology, paediatrics, education and economics – whose enquiries, outlining of evidence, and advocacy are providing powerful new support for the adoption of social democratic policies of the kind which the Nordic nations have developed and implemented most fully. The ideas of these experts offer an antidote to the despair and demoralisation which have become so common among Left-of-centre people put off by the cynical practices and superficiality of modern politics.

The support which these policy experts are now providing to social democratic approaches points to a need to revise past hostility to those characterised as 'technocrats' and to what is characterised as 'technocracy', or the rule of experts. Plutocracy, or government by the wealthy in their own self-interest, is now a far bigger threat to democracy and social democracy than is so-called technocracy.

---

1   Wilkinson and Pickett, *The Spirit Level*, pp. 75–76, 256.

There has though, very importantly, been a tradition in the Nordic social democratic nations of many people gaining knowledge and developing skills through activity in co-operatives, in community discussion groups, as rank-and-file members of trade unions in the workplace, and as part of education systems which themselves have been strongly influenced by the labour movement. This has fostered a political culture of democratic grass-roots participation in those countries. Part of that culture is the continuing very high and active membership of trade unions in the Nordic nations.

The Nordic nations' participatory political cultures are also reflected in the much higher membership of – and those members' much more meaningful activity in – their social democratic and labour parties compared with the Anglo-Australasian labour parties. The ALP, for example, is a relatively inward-looking, factionalised party dominated by machine organisational processes, which gives little space, respect or reason for the discussion or pursuit of policy ideas. Fostering a stronger culture of political participation will be necessary to achieve economic and social policy change towards a more egalitarian Australia. At the same time, further assembling and highlighting evidence from experts in relevant fields will also be essential to achieve that policy change.

The four main Nordic nations face a continuing challenge of their own to more fully and successfully 'integrate' immigrants into their generally very egalitarian provision of employment and other important life opportunities.

Some important examples and details of social democratic policies which the four principal Nordic nations have pursued, from which Australia can now learn, have been outlined in Chapters 2, 3, 4 and 5. Some tentative but important steps towards some of those policies have already been taken in Australia and – building on that beginning – some further and bigger steps can now be taken. I will now recap and briefly summarise the main points from each of those four chapters, in the next four paragraphs, prior to concluding this book.

Sweden is a country which has led the world in treating children with respect and dignity and which as a result leads the world in the equality and wellbeing which its children enjoy. Swedish society gives parents support, security and balance in their working lives, by regulating hours and by providing extensive paid parental leave. By doing this, Sweden enhances those parents' long-term workforce participation. Sweden also acts at all levels to prevent, and to regularly check on, the things which might harm children. It provides comprehensive, affordable and high quality ECEC from the first years of infancy. It highly and tangibly values its early childhood educators and carers. It focuses explicitly on gender equality. Together these approaches lead to healthier newborn babies whose nutritional needs are thoroughly met, who survive and thrive in their early years, and who then acquire a strong basis for learning. Australia has picked up some of these Swedish ECEC policies, and it can now pick up more, particularly by adopting new, place-based approaches in disadvantaged areas which feature multi-faceted child health, parenting and employment programs such as those pursued in Sweden.

Finland has rocketed to world leadership in educational quality and equity since the 1990s. One reason for this is Finland's building up, prior to then, of a genuinely comprehensive public school system. A second reason is Finland's high valuing of the profession of teaching. Finland shows how highly it regards teachers not only in its requirements for entry to the profession but also in the collegial daily working life, with ongoing opportunities for professional development, which it enables trusted teachers to experience in well-designed, well-resourced schools. A third reason for Finland's educational success is that it encourages students' learning and acts to ensure that every individual student's welfare and learning needs are met. This extends to encouraging those who pursue vocational, rather than more general academic, upper secondary education; and it extends to ensuring that those students are not disadvantaged by that very valid choice. Australia has taken some steps towards the Finnish approach, and away from its very socio-economically segregated mix of private and public schools, by its partial implementation of the recommendations of the Gonski Report. It can take further steps by now fully implementing the Gonski funding recommendations, by rearranging vocational education as a separate but equal and integral part of upper secondary schooling, and by improving the careers advice given in schools. Australia can also proceed closer to Finland's success by moving away from high-stakes testing, from unhealthy competition between schools and from erratic, partisan political interference in school curricula.

Denmark, like Australia, has a flexible workforce. However, unlike Australia, Denmark pays adequate unemployment benefits and invests substantially in ALMPs. Together, these give retrenched workers and other unemployed people the basis of security which they need to retrain to gain new skills and to make a transition into new jobs. The workforce – and especially prime-age workers facing the disaster of premature termination of their paid employment – will benefit from the introduction of more adequate unemployment benefits, and comprehensive ALMPs, in Australia. Policy makers in

Australia have started considering, through exploratory costings, an unemployment income insurance scheme. Australian trade unions and governments can now revisit and complete this work. Doing this will help to better meet the needs of those who are currently unemployed as well as the very many additional workers who are now facing job losses, to enable them to still be part of Australia's future workforce. Australia also needs to improve employment services to make them more positive. One part of this requires better recognition of unemployed people's skills gained from their prior learning and experience. Another part requires more intervention to ensure the matching of unemployed workers' skills to new job opportunities which arise, such as in new infrastructure projects. By taking such steps, Australia can reduce unemployment in the future towards the low rates which the Danes have consistently achieved. Efforts to create new employment-intensive projects in locations severely affected by economic change should also be made, drawing on Danish examples among others, in order to reduce the extent of Australia's regional inequalities.

Norway's taxation and regulation policies show Australia a better way for a nation to use and manage the products which result from its luck in having a valuable presence of sought-after natural resources. In Norway, the nation receives a fair share of the resources which belong to it while at the same time private sector companies are able to make a reasonable profit from their extraction. In Norway, concerted efforts have been made in connection with resource extraction to build up additional industries, jobs and infrastructure, and these are now flourishing. The revenue received by Norway from the taxation of its natural resource riches is used to support spending on socially and environmentally beneficial policies. That revenue is also managed in a way that assures the entire nation's long-term wealth. In Australia, there has already been recognition of the successful precedent of Norway's approach to resource taxation: in the Henry Report. That report deserves to be revived and more fully acted upon. The decision taken by the Abbott Government to further reduce what modest taxation there is of private sector resource-extraction companies operating in Australia must be reversed. This decision has put further strain on a public sector in Australia which is already under-resourced and it will further subtract from levels of government expenditure which are already inadequate. The support which some leading employers, among others, have shown for Australia to set up a fully fledged sovereign wealth fund, like that which Norway has, should now be consolidated into firm proposals so that Australia can invest more effectively for its future.

* * *

The policies pursued by Sweden, Finland, Denmark and Norway, as I have discussed them in this book, should now be actively regarded by all people who want greater prosperity, equality and sustainability, as live possibilities for Australia. Those nations together provide a positive policy example from which Australia and other English-speaking nations can now learn.

The Northern Lights pictured on the front cover of this book are, literally, the result of particles from the sun having their charge directed to the North Pole when they come into contact with Earth's magnetic field, which leads to a collision with atoms of oxygen and nitrogen. This generates the striking multicoloured, seemingly magical display across the dark night sky which can be seen from the northernmost parts of Sweden, Finland, Denmark and Norway due to the closeness of those countries to the North Pole.

There is an identical occurrence at the world's other extremity, the South Pole. However, the greater distance of Australia and other inhabited nations from the South Pole makes sightings of this much rarer.

Sweden, Finland, Denmark and Norway are 'Northern Lights', figuratively, because they offer distant but positive – indeed bright, shining – examples of how policies for economic prosperity, social equality and environmental responsibility can be combined. The light cast by the four main Nordic nations' achievements can inspire Australians, and people from other countries; and it can also help to guide them as they navigate to a better balance between those policies than they have so far been able to find.

INDEX

INDEX

INDEX